PENGUIN PLAYS

PL 17

ANNA CHRISTIE

THE EMPEROR JONES

DESIRE UNDER THE ELMS

EUGENE O'NEILL

EUGENE O'NEILL

Anna Christie
The Emperor Jones
Desire Under the Elms

INTRODUCED AND EDITED BY
E. MARTIN BROWNE

PENGUIN BOOKS

Penguin Books Ltd, Harmondsworth, Middlesex
AUSTRALIA: Penguin Books Pty Ltd, 762 Whitehorse Road,
Mitcham, Victoria

—

Chris Christopherson first performed 1920
First performed as *Anna Christie* 1921
Anna Christie first published 1922
First published in Great Britain by Cape 1923

The Emperor Jones first performed 1920
First published 1921
First published in Great Britain by Cape 1922

Desire Under the Elms first performed 1924
First published 1924
First published in Great Britain by Cape 1925

This collection first published in Penguin Books 1960

Made and printed in Great Britain
by Western Printing Services Ltd,
Bristol

CONTENTS

INTRODUCTION

Eugene O'Neill was born in New York on 16 October 1888. He was little more than thirty when he was recognized as America's leading dramatist. In the 1920s, that position was more significant than at any time before or since: for it was in those years that America achieved for the first time a drama truly her own. Up to the First World War, American writing for the stage was largely based upon European models; but after her great leap forward into power in that war, she produced a generation of writers who dramatized American life in an idiom and a language that belonged to it. Sidney Howard, George Kaufman, Robert Sherwood, Elmer Rice, Paul Green, Lilian Hellman are a few of the distinguished names among them. But Eugene O'Neill has a genius which places him above them all.

To European readers, this genius has certain forbidding aspects. It is violent, seldom relieved by humour. It is almost always concerned with life in the raw. His writing can appear turgid, even morbid. But a deeper acquaintance with it will prove this impression to be false. The low life in O'Neill's plays is drawn from experience; for until he was twenty-four, when the threat of tuberculosis and five months in a sanatorium changed his way of life and gave him time to discover that writing was his vocation, he had 'bummed' his way round much of the world by sea and land, living hard and desperately.

But this life in his plays is not only authentic; it is also continually touched with poetry. As a social rebel, O'Neill girded at those who were bound by convention and aimed at climbing the social ladder; they were blind, while those who lived at the bottom of the ladder were simple enough to look up through their misery and see the stars.

O'Neill was constantly experimenting with new forms of drama. By this means he made a further and very important contribution to the growth of the American theatre.

He was a voracious reader:

> I read about everything I could lay my hands on: the Greeks, the Elizabethans – practically all the classics – and of course all the moderns. Ibsen and Strindberg, especially Strindberg.

This is his own account at the time when he was beginning in earnest to write plays. The two Scandinavians and the German Wedekind were the most powerful influences on his mind. It is often said that he followed the German Expressionists of the early twenties – Toller and Kaiser; but in fact he had found for himself certain of their ideas. He always kept what they surrendered, the human individual as the mainspring of his drama; for him, man never became an abstract or a mechanical being.

In fact, his effort to free the theatre from outworn conventions of form took him in the opposite direction. Already, in one of his early one-act plays, *The Moon of the Caribees*, he dispenses almost entirely with plot, in order to allow his principal character to reveal himself by speaking his dreams aloud.

Here also we can already listen to that strongly rhythmic prose which he develops as he gains confidence. It is the right vehicle to convey the universalized characters who march through the following plays. *The Emperor Jones, The Hairy Ape, The Great God Brown*, each becomes more boldly experimental, until as the twenties draw to a close the marathon *Strange Interlude* raises the old convention of the 'aside' to its *n*th power.

Like all good rebels, O'Neill started with a first-hand knowledge of what he was rebelling against. His father, James O'Neill, was an accomplished actor of the old school. By the time Eugene was grown up, James had found in *Monte Cristo* a 'surefire' vehicle which ruined his art by allowing it to become a routine. Eugene occasionally toured with him and played small parts, and when in 1913 he knew his destiny as a playwright he had soaked himself in the ways and tricks of the old-fashioned theatre. (His own account of the family's life is given with masterly power in *Long Day's Journey into Night*.)

So anti-conventional a dramatist could not find his way directly on to Broadway. It was to the Provincetown Players under George Cram Cook that he owed his first productions. Most of his plays until the middle twenties had their first showing in Greenwich Village under Cook. Since then, he has come to occupy a position in America not unlike that of G.B.S. in England: the young rebel has become the Old Master. Of the plays written in the years immediately preceding his death in 1953, two very long ones, *The Iceman Cometh* and *Long Day's Journey*, have made the most sustained impact.

In this first volume we have three plays all dating from the early twenties. *Anna Christie* was first seen in a version entitled *Chris Christopherson* in 1920. As the two titles indicate, O'Neill changed it from a play about a man to a play about his daughter. Chris, the captain of the coal barge, is founded on a real character who was O'Neill's room-mate at Jimmy-the-Priest's, a verminous waterfront dive in New York where he lived in 1911 for $3.00 a month.

> He had sailed the sea until he was sick of the mention of it. But it was the only work he knew. At the time he was my room-mate he was out of work, wouldn't go to sea and spent the time guzzling whisky and razzing the sea.

This is O'Neill's description of him (quoted from an article in the *New York Times*, 21 December 1924). Chris's famous phrase 'Dat ole Davil sea' provided the original theme of the play. As such, Chris's insistence on it did not appear excessive; but since Chris has taken second place, in *Anna Christie*, he seems to labour the subject. Anna's story has become the centre of the play, which is a moving one. But her character is not wholly convincing; the girl whom we first meet as a harlot turns out to be really 'pure in soul' all the time, and the ending becomes sentimental theatre rather than the outcome of a real change in herself. But despite its faults the play is one of O'Neill's best-loved works.

The Emperor Jones is the first major example of that simplification on to a single theme which we have noted as O'Neill's brand of Expressionism. It exhibits the power of O'Neill's rhythm, with the drums as ground-bass; the evocation of the noble savage, and of the effect of primitive terror upon him, is haunting. It is a short play, confined to one cumulative effect; but it does superbly what it sets out to do.

Desire Under the Elms (1924) is a much subtler work, one of the playwright's finest creations. It is a tragedy, according to the strict definition of that word, and has the cathartic effect that Aristotle associated with tragedy. Ephraim, the father and owner of the farm, is a figure of tragic stature, breeding his downfall by his own pride, yet expressing in himself the permanent values for which he stands. Against him are set the young and passionate lovers, whose love is bound up with the land-hunger which motivates Ephraim, but is finally released from it. The play is firmly constructed, and unified within a multiple set showing the whole of the house which is the symbol of possession; one is reminded of Hauptmann's *The Weavers* by this experiment. This play may be reckoned one of the first classics to be produced by the American theatre.

*Complete list of O'Neill plays and years
in which they were written*

—

1913
THE WEB

1914
THIRST — RECKLESSNESS — WARNING
BOUND EAST FOR CARDIFF
FOG — SERVITUDE — A WIFE FOR A LIFE
THE MOVIE MAN — ABORTION

1915
A KNOCK AT THE DOOR — THE SNIPER
BELTHAZAR — THE DEAR DOCTOR
THE SECOND ENGINEER

1916
THE LONG VOYAGE HOME
IN THE ZONE — ILE
THE MOON OF THE CARIBBEES (S.S. GLENCAIRN)
BEFORE BREAKFAST

1918
BEYOND THE HORIZON — THE STRAW
WHERE THE CROSS IS MADE — THE DREAMY KID
SHELL SHOP — TILL WE MEET — THE ROPE

1919
HONOUR AMONG THE BRADLEYS — THE TRUMPET
EXORCISM — CHRIS CHRISTOPHERSON

1920
DIFF'RENT — THE EMPEROR JONES
GOLD — ANNA CHRISTIE

ANNA CHRISTIE

CHARACTERS

'Johnny-the-Priest'
Two Longshoremen
A Postman
Larry, Bar-tender
Chris Christopherson, Captain of the barge *Simeon Winthrop*
Marthy Owen
Anna Christopherson, Chris's daughter
Three Men of a Steamer's Crew
Mat Burke, a Stoker
Johnson, Deckhand on the barge

SCENES

ACT I

'Johnny-the-Priest's' saloon near the water-front, New York City

ACT II

The barge, *Simeon Winthrop*, at anchor in the harbour of Provincetown, Mass. Ten days later

ACT III

Cabin of the barge, at dock in Boston. A week later

ACT IV

The same. Two days later

Time of the Play – About 1910

ACT ONE

'Johnny-the-Priest's' saloon near South Street, New York City. The stage is divided into two sections, showing a small back room on the right. On the left, forward, of the bar-room, a large window looking out on the street. Beyond it, the main entrance – a double swinging door. Farther back, another window. The bar runs from left to right nearly the whole length of the rear wall. In back of the bar, a small showcase displaying a few bottles of goods, for which there is evidently little call. The remainder of the rear space in front of the large mirrors is occupied by half-barrels of cheap whisky of the 'nickel-a-shot' variety, from which the liquor is drawn by means of spigots. On the right is an open doorway leading to the back room. In the back room are four round wooden tables with five chairs grouped about each. In the rear, a family entrance opening on a side street.

It is late afternoon of a day in autumn.

[As the curtain rises, JOHNNY *is discovered.* 'JOHNNY-THE-PRIEST' *deserves his nickname. With his pale, thin, clean-shaven face, mild blue eyes, and white hair, a cassock would seem more suited to him than the apron he wears. Neither his voice nor his general manner dispels this illusion which has made him a personage of the water-front. They are soft and bland. But beneath all his mildness one senses the man behind the mask – cynical, callous, hard as nails. He is lounging at ease behind the bar, a pair of spectacles on his nose, reading an evening paper.*

Two longshoremen enter from the street, wearing their working aprons, the button of the Union pinned conspicuously on the caps pulled sideways on their heads at an aggressive angle.]

FIRST LONGSHOREMAN [*as they range themselves at the bar*]: Gimme a shock. Number Two. [*He tosses a coin on the bar.*]

SECOND LONGSHOREMAN: Same here.

[JOHNNY *sets two glasses of barrel whisky before them.*]

FIRST LONGSHOREMAN: Here's luck!

[*The other nods. They gulp down their whisky.*]

SECOND LONGSHOREMAN [*putting money on the bar*]: Give us another.

FIRST LONGSHOREMAN: Gimme a scoop this time – lager and porter. I'm dry.

SECOND LONGSHOREMAN: Same here.

[JOHNNY *draws the lager and porter and sets the big, foaming tankards before them. They drink down half the contents and start to talk together hurriedly in low tones. The door on the left is swung open and* LARRY *enters. He is a boyish, red-cheeked, rather good-looking young fellow of twenty or so.*]

LARRY [*nodding to* JOHNNY – *cheerily*]: Hallo, boss!

JOHNNY: Hallo, Larry! [*With a glance at his watch*] Just on time.

[LARRY *goes to the right, behind the bar, takes off his coat, and puts on an apron.*]

FIRST LONGSHOREMAN [*abruptly*]: Let's drink up and get back to it.

[*They finish their drinks and go out left.* THE POSTMAN *enters as they leave. He exchanges nods with* JOHNNY *and throws a letter on the bar.*]

THE POSTMAN: Addressed care of you, Johnny. Know him?

JOHNNY [*picks up the letter, adjusting his spectacles.* LARRY *comes and peers over his shoulder.* JOHNNY *reads very slowly*]: Christopher Christopherson.

THE POSTMAN [*helpfully*]: Square-head name.

LARRY: Old Chris – that's who.

JOHNNY: Oh, sure. I was forgetting Chris carried a hell of a name like that. Letters come here for him sometimes before, I remember now. Long time ago, though.

THE POSTMAN: It'll get him all right, then?

JOHNNY: Sure thing. He comes here whenever he's in port.

THE POSTMAN [*turning to go*]: Sailor, eh?

JOHNNY [*with a grin*]: Captain of a coal barge.

THE POSTMAN [*laughing*]: Some job! Well, s'long.

JOHNNY: S'long. I'll see he gets it. [THE POSTMAN *goes out.* JOHNNY *scrutinizes the letter.*] You got good eyes, Larry. Where's it from?

LARRY [*after a glance*]: St Paul. That'll be in Minnesota, I'm thinkin'. Looks like a woman's writing, too, the old divil!

JOHNNY: He's got a daughter somewheres out West, I think he told me once. [*He puts the letter on the cash register.*] Come to think of it, I ain't seen old Chris in a dog's age. [*Putting his overcoat on, he comes around the end of the bar.*] Guess I'll be gettin' home. See you tomorrow.

LARRY: Good night to ye, boss.

[*As* JOHNNY *goes toward the street door, it is pushed open and* CHRISTOPHER CHRISTOPHERSON *enters. He is a short, squat, broad-shouldered man of about fifty, with a round, weather-beaten, red face from which his light-blue eyes peer short-sightedly, twinkling with a simple good humour. His large mouth, overhung by a thick, drooping, yellow moustache, is childishly self-willed and weak, of an obstinate kindliness. A thick neck is jammed like a post into the heavy trunk of his body. His arms, with their big, hairy, freckled hands, and his stumpy legs terminating in large, flat feet, are awkwardly short and muscular. He walks with a clumsy, rolling gait. His voice, when not raised in a hollow boom, is toned down to a sly, confidential half-whisper with something vaguely plaintive in its quality. He is dressed in a wrinkled, ill-fitting, dark suit of shore clothes, and wears a faded cap of grey cloth over his mop of grizzled, blond hair. Just now his face beams with a too-blissful happiness, and he has evidently been drinking. He reaches his hand out to* JOHNNY.]

CHRIS: Hallo, Yohnny! Have drink on me. Come on, Larry. Give us drink. Have one yourself. [*Putting his hand in his pocket*] Ay gat money – plenty money.

17

JOHNNY [*shakes* CHRIS *by the hand*]: Speak of the devil. We was just talkin' about you.

LARRY [*coming to the end of the bar*]: Hallo, Chris! Put it there. [*They shake hands.*]

CHRIS [*beaming*]: Give us drink.

JOHNNY [*with a grin*]: You got a half-snootful now. Where'd you get it?

CHRIS [*grinning*]: Oder fallar on oder barge – Irish fallar – he gat bottle vhisky and we drank it, yust us two. Dot vhisky get kick, by yingo! Ay yust come ashore. Give us drink, Larry, Ay vas little drunk, not much. Yust feel good. [*He laughs and commences to sing in a nasal, high-pitched quaver:*]

'My Yosephine, come board de ship. Long time Ay vait for you.

De moon, she shi-i-i-ine. She looka yust like you.

Tchee-tchee, tchee-tchee, tchee-tchee, tchee-tchee.'

[*To the accompaniment of this last he waves his hand as if he were conducting an orchestra.*]

JOHNNY [*with a laugh*]: Same old Yosie, eh, Chris?

CHRIS: You don't know good song when you hear him. Italian fallar on oder barge, he learn me dat. Give us drink. [*He throws change on the bar.*]

LARRY [*with a professional air*]: What's your pleasure, gentlemen?

JOHNNY: Small beer, Larry.

CHRIS: Vhisky – Number Two.

LARRY [*as he gets their drinks*]: I'll take a cigar on you.

CHRIS [*lifting his glass*]: Skoal! [*He drinks.*]

JOHNNY: Drink hearty.

CHRIS [*immediately*]: Have oder drink.

JOHNNY: No. Some other time. Got to go home now. So you've just landed? Where are you in from this time?

CHRIS: Norfolk. Ve make slow voyage – dirty vedder – yust fog, fog, fog, all bloody time! [*There is an insistent ring from the door-bell at the family entrance in the back room.* CHRIS *gives a start – hurriedly*] Ay go open, Larry. Ay forgat. It vas Marthy. She come with me. [*He goes into the back room.*]

LARRY [*with a chuckle*]: He's still got that same cow livin' with him, the old fool!

JOHNNY [*with a grin*]: A sport, Chris is. Well, I'll beat it home. S'long. [*He goes to the street door.*]

LARRY: So long, boss.

JOHNNY: Oh – don't forget to give him his letter.

LARRY: I won't.

[JOHNNY *goes out. In the meantime,* CHRIS *has opened the family entrance door, admitting* MARTHY. *She might be forty or fifty. Her jowly, mottled face, with its thick, red nose, is streaked with interlacing purple veins. Her thick, grey hair is piled anyhow in a greasy mop on top of her round head. Her figure is flabby and fat; her breath comes in wheezy gasps; she speaks in a loud, mannish voice, punctuated by explosions of hoarse laughter. But there still twinkles in her blood-shot blue eyes a youthful lust for life which hard usage has failed to stifle, a sense of humour, mocking, but good-tempered. She wears a man's cap, double-breasted man's jacket, and a grimy, calico skirt. Her bare feet are encased in a man's shoes several sizes too large for her, which gives her a shuffling, wobbly gait.*]

MARTHY [*grumblingly*]: What yuh tryin' to do, Dutchy – keep me standin' out there all day? [*She comes forward and sits at the table in the right corner, front.*]

CHRIS [*mollifyingly*]: Ay'm sorry, Marthy. Ay talk to Yohnny. Ay forgat. What you goin' take for drink?

MARTHY [*appeased*]: Gimme a scoop of lager an' ale.

CHRIS: Ay go bring him back. [*He returns to the bar.*] Lager and ale for Marthy, Larry. Vhisky for me. [*He throws change on the bar.*]

LARRY: Right you are. [*Then remembering, he takes the letter from in back of the bar.*] Here's a letter for you – from St Paul, Minnesota – and a lady's writin'. [*He grins.*]

CHRIS [*quickly – taking it*]: Oh, den it co e from my daughter, Anna. She live dere. [*He turns the l er over in his hands uncertainly.*] Ay don't gat letter from Anna – must be a year.

LARRY [*jokingly*]: That's a fine fairy tale to be tellin' – your daughter! Sure, I'll bet it's some tart.

CHRIS [*soberly*]: No. Dis come from Anna. [*Engrossed by the letter in his hand – uncertainly*] By golly, Ay tank Ay'm too drunk for read dis letter from Anna. Ay tank Ay sat down for a minute. You bring drinks in back room, Larry. [*He goes into the room on right.*]

MARTHY [*angrily*]: Where's my lager an' ale, yuh big stiff?

CHRIS [*preoccupied*]: Larry bring him.

[*He sits down opposite her.* LARRY *brings in the drinks and sets them on the table. He and* MARTHY *exchange nods of recognition.* LARRY *stands looking at* CHRIS *curiously.* MARTHY *takes a long draught of her tankard and heaves a huge sigh of satisfaction, wiping her mouth with the back of her hand.* CHRIS *stares at the letter for a moment – slowly opens it, and squinting his eyes, commences to read laboriously, his lips moving as he spells out the words. As he reads his face lights up with an expression of mingled joy and bewilderment.*]

LARRY: Good news?

MARTHY [*her curiosity also aroused*]: What's that yuh got – a letter, fur Gawd's sake?

CHRIS [*pauses for a moment, after finishing the letter, as if to let the news sink in – then suddenly pounds his fist on the table with happy excitement*]: Py yiminy! Yust tank, Anna say she's comin' here right avay! She gat sick on yob in St Paul, she say. It's short letter, don't tal me much more'n dat. [*Beaming*] Py golly, dat's good news all at one time for ole fallar! [*Then turning to* MARTHY, *rather shamefacedly*] You know, Marthy, Ay've tole you Ay don't see my Anna since she vas little gel in Sveden five year ole.

MARTHY: How old'll she be now?

CHRIS: She must be – lat me see – she must be twenty year ole, py Yo!

LARRY [*surprised*]: You've not seen her in fifteen years?

CHRIS [*suddenly growing sombre – in a low tone*]: No. Ven she vas little gel, Ay vas bo'sun on vindyammer. Ay never gat home only few time dem year. Ay'm fool sailor fallar. My voman – Anna's mother – she gat tired vait all time Sveden for me ven Ay don't never come. She come dis country, bring Anna, dey go out Minnesota, live with her cousins on farm. Den ven her mo'der die ven Ay vas on voyage, Ay tank it's better dem cousins keep Anna. Ay tank it's better Anna live on farm, den she don't know dat ole davil, sea, she don't know fader like me.

LARRY [*with a wink at* MARTHY]: This girl, now'll be marryin' a sailor herself, likely. It's in the blood.

CHRIS [*suddenly springing to his feet and smashing his fist on the table in a rage*]: No, py God! She don't do dat!

MARTHY [*grasping her tankard hastily – angrily*]: Hey, look out, yuh nut! Wanta spill my suds for me?

LARRY [*amazed*]: Oho, what's up with you? Ain't you a sailor yourself now, and always been?

CHRIS [*slowly*]: Dat's yust vhy Ay say it. [*Forcing a smile*] Sailor vas all right fallar, but not for marry gel. No. Ay know dat. Anna's mo'der, she know it, too.

LARRY [*as* CHRIS *remains sunk in gloomy reflection*]: When is your daughter comin'? Soon?

CHRIS [*roused*]: Py yiminy, Ay forgat. [*Reads through the letter hurriedly.*] She say she come right avay, dat's all.

LARRY: She'll maybe be comin' here to look for you, I s'pose. [*He returns to the bar, whistling. Left alone with* MARTHY, *who stares at him with a twinkle of malicious humour in her eyes,* CHRIS *suddenly becomes desperately ill at ease. He fidgets, then gets up hurriedly.*]

CHRIS: Ay gat speak with Larry. Ay be right back. [*Mollifyingly*] Ay bring you oder drink.

MARTHY [*emptying her glass*]: Sure. That's me. [*As he retreats with the glass she guffaws after him derisively.*]

CHRIS [*to* LARRY *in an alarmed whisper*]: Py yingo, Ay gat gat Marthy shore off barge before Anna come! Anna raise hell if she find dat out. Marthy raise hell, too, for go, py golly!

LARRY [*with a chuckle*]: Serve ye right, ye old divil – havin' a woman at your age!

CHRIS [*scratching his head in a quandary*]: You tal me lie for tal Marthy, Larry, so's she gat off barge quick.

LARRY: She knows your daughter's comin'. Tell her to get the hell out of it.

CHRIS: No. Ay don't like make her feel bad.

LARRY: You're an old mush! Keep your girl away from the barge, then. She'll likely want to stay ashore, anyway. [*Curiously*] What does she work at, your Anna?

CHRIS: She stay on dem cousins' farm till two year ago. Dan she gat yob nurse gel in St Paul. [*Then shaking his head resolutely*] But Ay don't vant for her gat yob now. Ay vant for her stay with me.

LARRY [*scornfully*]: On a coal barge! She'll not like that, I'm thinkin'.

MARTHY [*shouts from next room*]: Don't I get that bucket o' suds, Dutchy?

CHRIS [*startled – in apprehensive confusion*]: Yes, Ay come, Marthy.

LARRY [*drawing the lager and ale, hands it to* CHRIS – *laughing*]: Now you're in for it! You'd better tell her straight to get out!

CHRIS [*shaking in his boots*]: Py golly. [*He takes her drink in to* MARTHY *and sits down at the table. She sips it in silence.* LARRY *moves quietly close to the partition to listen, grinning with expectation.* CHRIS *seems on the verge of speaking, hesitates, gulps down his whisky desperately as if seeking for courage. He attempts to whistle a few bars of 'Yosephine' with careless bravado, but the whistle peters out futilely.* MARTHY *stares at him keenly, taking in his embarrassment with a malicious twinkle of amusement in her eye.* CHRIS *clears his throat.*] Marthy –

MARTHY [*aggressively*]: Wha's that? [*Then, pretending to fly into a rage, her eyes enjoying* CHRIS'S *misery*] I'm wise to what's in back of your nut, Dutchy. Yuh want to git rid o' me, huh? – now she's comin'. Gimme the rush ashore, huh? Lemme tell yuh, Dutchy, there ain't a square-head workin' on a boat man enough to git away with that. Don't start nothin' yuh can't finish!

CHRIS [*miserably*]: Ay don't start nutting, Marthy.

MARTHY [*glares at him for a second – then cannot control a burst of laughter*]: Ho-ho! Yuh're a scream, Square-head – an honest-ter-Gawd knock-out! Ho-ho! [*She wheezes, panting for breath.*]

CHRIS [*with childish pique*]: Ay don't see nutting for laugh at.

MARTHY: Take a slant in the mirror and yuh'll see. Ho-ho! [*Recovering from her mirth – chuckling, scornfully*] A square-head tryin' to kid Marthy Owen at this late day! – after me campin' with barge-men the last twenty years. I'm wise to the game, up, down, and sideways. I ain't been born and dragged up on the water-front for nothin'. Think I'd make trouble, huh? Not me! I'll pack up me duds an' beat it. I'm quittin' yuh, get me? I'm tellin' yuh I'm sick of stickin' with yuh, and I'm leavin' yuh flat, see? There's plenty of other guys on other barges waitin' for me. Always was, I always found. [*She claps the astonished* CHRIS *on the back.*] So cheer up, Dutchy! I'll be offen the barge before she comes. You'll be rid o' me for good – and me o' you – good riddance for both of us. Ho-ho!

CHRIS [*seriously*]: Ay don' tank dat. You vas good gel, Marthy.

MARTHY [*grinning*]: Good girl? Aw, can the bull! Well, yuh treated me square, yuhself. So it's fifty-fifty. Nobody's sore at nobody. We're still good frien's, huh?

[LARRY *returns to bar.*]

CHRIS [*beaming now that he sees his troubles disappearing*]: Yes, py golly.

MARTHY: That's the talkin'! In all my time I tried never to split with a guy with no hard feelin's. But what was yuh so scared about – that I'd kick up a row? That ain't Marthy's way. [*Scornfully*] Think I'd break my heart to loose yuh? Commit suicide, huh? Ho-ho! Gawd! The world's full o' men if that's all I'd worry about! [*Then with a grin, after emptying her glass*] Blow me to another scoop, huh? I'll drink your kid's health for yuh.

CHRIS [*eagerly*]: Sure tang. Ay go gat him. [*He takes the two glasses into the bar.*] Oder drink. Same for both.

LARRY [*getting the drinks and putting them on the bar*]: She's not such a bad lot, that one.

CHRIS [*jovially*]: She's good gel, Ay tal you! Py golly, Ay calabrate now! Give me vhisky here at bar, too. [*He puts down money. LARRY serves him.*] You have drink, Larry?

LARRY [*virtuously*]: You know I never touch it.

CHRIS: You don't know what you miss. Skoal! [*He drinks – then begins to sing loudly:*]
'My Yosephine, come board de ship – '
[*He picks up the drinks for MARTHY and himself and walks unsteadily into the back room, singing:*]
'De moon she shi-i-i-ine. She looks yust like you.
Tchee-tchee, tchee-tchee, tchee-tchee, tchee-tchee.'

MARTHY [*grinning, hands to ears*]: Gawd!

CHRIS [*sitting down*]: Ay'm good singer, yes? Ve drink, eh? Skoal! Ay calabrate! [*He drinks.*] Ay calabrate 'cause Anna's coming home. You know, Marthy, Ay never write for her to come, 'cause Ay tank Ay'm no good for her. But all time Ay hope like hell some day she vant for see me and den she come. And dat's vay it happen now, py yiminy! [*His face beaming*] What you tank she look like, Marthy? Ay bet you she's fine, good, strong gel, pooty like hell! Living on farm made her like dat. And Ay bet you some day she marry

24

good, steady land fallar here in East, have home all her own, have kits – and dan Ay'm ole grandfader, py golly! And Ay go visit dem every time Ay gat in port near! [*Bursting with joy*] By yiminy crickens, Ay calabrate dat! [*Shouts*] Bring oder drink, Larry! [*He smashes his fist on the table with a bang.*]

LARRY [*coming in from bar – irritably*]: Easy there! Don't be breakin' the table, you old goat!

CHRIS [*by way of reply, grins foolishly and begins to sing*]: 'My Yosephine comes board de ship – '

MARTHY [*touching* CHRIS's *arm persuasively*]: You're soused to the ears, Dutchy. Go out and put a feed into you. It'll sober you up. [*Then as* CHRIS *shakes his head obstinately*] Listen, yuh old nut! Yuh don't know what time your kid's liable to show up. Yuh want to be sober when she comes, don't yuh?

CHRIS [*aroused – gets unsteadily to his feet*]: Py golly, yes.

LARRY: That's good sense for you. A good beef stew'll fix you. Go round the corner.

CHRIS: All right. Ay be back soon, Marthy. [CHRIS *goes through the bar and out the street door.*]

LARRY: He'll come round all right with some grub in him.

MARTHY: Sure.

[LARRY *goes back to the bar and resumes his newspaper.* MARTHY *sips what is left of her tankard reflectively. There is the ring of the family entrance bell.* LARRY *comes to the door and opens it a trifle – then, with a puzzled expression, pulls it wide.* ANNA CHRISTOPHERSON *enters. She is a tall, blonde, fully developed girl of twenty, handsome after a large, Viking-daughter fashion, but now run down in health and plainly showing all the outward evidences of belonging to the world's oldest profession. Her youthful face is already hard and cynical beneath its layer of make-up. Her clothes are the tawdry finery of peasant stock turned prostitute. She comes and sinks wearily in a chair by the table, left front.*]

ANNA: Gimme a whisky – ginger ale on the side. [*Then, as* LARRY *turns to go, forcing a winning smile at him*] And don't be stingy, baby.

LARRY [*sarcastically*]: Shall I serve it in a pail?

ANNA [*with a hard laugh*]: That suits me down to the ground. [LARRY *goes into the bar. The two women size each other up with frank stares.* LARRY *comes back with the drink, which he sets before* ANNA, *and returns to the bar again.* ANNA *downs her drink at a gulp. Then, after a moment, as the alcohol begins to rouse her, she turns to* MARTHY *with a friendly smile.*] Gee, I needed that bad, all right, all right!

MARTHY [*nodding her head sympathetically*]: Sure – yuh look all in. Been on a bat?

ANNA: No – travelling – day and a half on the train. Had to sit up all night in the dirty coach too. Gawd, I thought I'd never get here!

MARTHY [*with a start – looking at her intently*]: Where'd yuh come from, huh?

ANNA: St Paul – out in Minnesota.

MARTHY [*staring at her in amazement – slowly*]: So – yuh're – [*She suddenly bursts out into hoarse, ironical laughter.*] Gawd!

ANNA: All the way from Minnesota, sure. [*Flaring up*] What you laughing at? Me?

MARTHY [*hastily*]: No, honest, kid. I was thinkin' of somethin' else.

ANNA [*mollified – with a smile*]: Well, I wouldn't blame you, at that. Guess I do look rotten – yust out of the hospital two weeks. I'm going to have another 'ski. What d'you say? Have something on me?

MARTHY: Sure I will. T'anks. [*She calls*] Hey, Larry! Little service! [*He comes in.*]

ANNA: Same for me.

MARTHY: Same here.

[LARRY *takes their glasses and goes out.*]

ANNA: Why don't you come sit over here, be sociable. I'm a

dead stranger in this burg – and I ain't spoke a word with no one since day before yesterday.

MARTHY: Sure thing.

[*She shuffles over to* ANNA'S *table and sits down opposite her.* LARRY *brings the drinks and* ANNA *pays him.*]

ANNA: Skoal! Here's how! [*She drinks.*]

MARTHY: Here's luck! [*She takes a gulp from her tankard.*]

ANNA [*taking a package of Sweet Caporal cigarettes from her bag*]: Let you smoke in here, won't they?

MARTHY [*doubtfully*]: Sure. [*Then with evident anxiety*] On'y trow it away if yuh hear some one comin'.

ANNA [*lighting one and taking a deep inhale*]: Gee, they're fussy in this dump, ain't they? [*She puffs, staring at the table top.* MARTHY *looks her over with a new penetrating interest, taking in every detail of her face.* ANNA *suddenly becomes conscious of this appraising stare – resentfully*] Ain't nothing wrong with me, is there? You're looking hard enough.

MARTHY [*irritated by the other's tone – scornfully*]: Ain't got to look much. I got your number the minute you stepped in the door.

ANNA [*her eyes narrowing*]: Ain't you smart! Well, I got yours, too, without no trouble. You're me forty years from now. That's you! [*She gives a hard little laugh.*]

MARTHY [*angrily*]: Is that so? Well, I'll tell you straight, kiddo, that Marthy Owen never – [*She catches herself up short – with a grin.*] What are you and me scrappin' over? Let's cut it out, huh? Me, I don't want no hard feelin's with no one. [*Extending her hand*] Shake and forget it, huh?

ANNA [*shakes her hand gladly*]: Only too glad to. I ain't looking for trouble. Let's have 'nother. What d'you say?

MARTHY [*shaking her head*]: Not for mine. I'm full up. And you – had anythin' to eat lately?

ANNA: Not since this morning on the train.

MARTHY: Then yuh better go easy on it, hadn't yuh?

ANNA [*after a moment's hesitation*]: Guess you're right. I got to meet some one, too. But my nerves is on edge after that rotten trip.

MARTHY: Yuh said yuh was just outa the hospital?

ANNA: Two weeks ago. [*Leaning over to* MARTHY *confidentially*] The joint I was in out in St Paul got raided. That was the start. The judge give all us girls thirty days. The others didn't seem to mind being in the cooler much. Some of 'em was used to it. But me, I couldn't stand it. It got my goat right – couldn't eat or sleep or nothing. I never could stand being caged up nowheres. I got good and sick and they had to send me to the hospital. It was nice there. I was sorry to leave it, honest!

MARTHY [*after a slight pause*]: Did yuh say yuh got to meet some one here?

ANNA: Yes. Oh, not what you mean. It's my Old Man I got to meet. Honest! It's funny, too. I ain't seen him since I was a kid – don't even know what he looks like – yust had a letter every now and then. This was always the only address he give me to write him back. He's yanitor of some building here now – used to be a sailor.

MARTHY [*astonished*]: Janitor!

ANNA: Sure. And I was thinking maybe, seeing he ain't never done a thing for me in my life, he might be willing to stake me to a room and eats till I get rested up. [*Wearily*] Gee, I sure need that rest! I'm knocked out. [*Then resignedly*] But I ain't expecting much from him. Give you a kick when you're down, that's what all men do. [*With sudden passion*] Men, I hate 'em – all of 'em! And I don't expect he'll turn out no better than the rest. [*Then with sudden interest*] Say, do you hang out around this dump much?

MARTHY: Oh, off and on.

ANNA: Then maybe you know him – my Old Man – or at least seen him?

MARTHY: It ain't old Chris, is it?

ANNA: Old Chris?

MARTHY: Chris Christopherson, his full name is.

ANNA [*excitedly*]: Yes, that's him! Anna Christopherson – that's my real name – only out there I called myself Anna Christie. So you know him, eh?

MARTHY [*evasively*]: Seen him about for years.

ANNA: Say, what's he like, tell me – honest?

MARTHY: Oh, he's short and –

ANNA [*impatiently*]: I don't care what he looks like. What kind is he?

MARTHY [*earnestly*]: Well, yuh can bet your life, kid, he's as good an old guy as ever walked on two feet. That goes!

ANNA [*pleased*]: I'm glad to hear it. Then you thinks he'll stake me to that rest cure I'm after?

MARTHY [*emphatically*]: Surest thing you know. [*Disgustedly*] But where'd yuh get the idea he was a janitor?

ANNA: He wrote me he was himself.

MARTHY: Well, he was lyin'. He ain't. He's captain of a barge – five men under him.

ANNA [*disgusted in her turn*]: A barge? What kind of a barge?

MARTHY: Coal, mostly.

ANNA: A coal barge! [*With a harsh laugh*] If that ain't a swell job to find your long-lost Old Man working at! Gee, I knew something'd be bound to turn out wrong – always does with me. That puts my idea of his giving me a rest up the spout.

MARTHY: What d'yuh mean?

ANNA: I s'pose he lives on the boat, don't he?

MARTHY: Sure. What about it? Can't you live on it, too?

ANNA [*scornfully*]: Me? On a dirty coal barge! What d'you think I am?

MARTHY [*resentfully*]: What d'yuh know about barges, huh? Bet yuh ain't never seen one. That's what comes of his bringing yuh up inland – away from the old divil sea – where yuh'd be safe – Gawd! [*The irony of it strikes her sense of humour and she laughs hoarsely.*]

ANNA [angrily]: His bringing me up! Is that what he tells people! I like his nerve! He let them cousins of my Old Woman's keep me on their farm and work me to death like a dog.

MARTHY: Well, he's got queer notions on some things. I've heard him say a farm was the best place for a kid.

ANNA: Sure. That's what he'd always answer back – and a lot of crazy stuff about staying away from the sea – stuff I couldn't make head or tail to. I thought he must be nutty.

MARTHY: He is on that one point. [Casually] So yuh didn't fall for life on the farm, huh?

ANNA: I should say not! The old man of the family, his wife, and four sons – I had to slave for all of 'em. I was only a poor relation, and they treated me worse than they dare treat a hired girl. [After a moment's hesitation – sombrely] It was one of the sons – the youngest – started me – when I was sixteen. After that, I hated 'em so I'd killed 'em all if I'd stayed. So I run away – to St Paul.

MARTHY [who has been listening sympathetically]: I've heard Old Chris talkin' about your bein' a nurse girl out there. Was that all a bluff yuh put up when yuh wrote him?

ANNA: Not on your life, it wasn't. It was true for two years. I didn't go wrong all at one jump. Being a nurse girl was yust what finished me. Taking care of other people's kids, always listening to their bawling and crying, caged in, when you're only a kid yourself and want to go out and see things. At last I got the chance – to get into that house. And you bet your life I took it! [Defiantly] And I ain't sorry neither. [After a pause – with bitter hatred] It was all men's fault – the whole business. It was men on the farm ordering and beating me – and giving me the wrong start. Then when I was a nurse, it was men again hanging around, bothering me, trying to see what they could get. [She gives a hard laugh.] And now it's men all the time. Gawd, I hate 'em all, every mother's son of 'em! Don't you?

MARTHY: Oh, I dunno. There's good ones and bad ones, kid. You've just had a run of bad luck with 'em, that's all. Your Old Man, now – old Chris – he's a good one.

ANNA [*sceptically*]: He'll have to show me.

MARTHY: Yuh kept right on writing him yuh was a nurse girl still, even after yuh was in the house, didn't yuh?

ANNA: Sure. [*Cynically*] Not that I think he'd care a darn.

MARTHY: Yuh're all wrong about him, kid. [*Earnestly*] I know Old Chris well for a long time. He's talked to me 'bout you lots o' times. He thinks the world o' you, honest he does.

ANNA: Aw, quit the kiddin'!

MARTHY: Honest! Only, he's a simple old guy, see? He's got nutty notions. But he means well, honest. Listen to me, kid – [*She is interrupted by the opening and shutting of the street door in the bar and by hearing* CHRIS'S *voice.*] Ssshh!

ANNA: What's up?

CHRIS [*who has entered the bar. He seems considerably sobered up*]: Py golly, Larry, dat grub taste good. Marthy in back?

LARRY: Sure – and another tramp with her.

[CHRIS *starts for the entrance to the back room.*]

MARTHY [*to* ANNA *in a hurried, nervous whisper*]: That's him now. He's comin' in here. Brace up!

ANNA: Who?

[CHRIS *opens the door.*]

MARTHY [*as if she were greeting him for the first time*]: Why hallo, Old Chris. [*Then before he can speak, she shuffles hurriedly past him into the bar, beckoning him to follow her.*] Come here. I wanta tell yuh somethin'. [*He goes out to her. She speaks hurriedly in a low voice.*] Listen! I'm goin' to beat it down to the barge – pack up me duds and blow. That's her in there – your Anna – just come – waitin' for yuh. Treat her right, see? She's been sick. Well, s'long! [*She goes into the back room – to* ANNA.] S'long, kid. I gotta beat it now. See yuh later.

ANNA [*nervously*]: So long.

[MARTHY *goes quickly out of the family entrance.*]

LARRY [*looking at the stupefied* CHRIS *curiously*]: Well, what's up now?

CHRIS [*vaguely*]: Nutting – nutting. [*He stands before the door to the back room in an agony of embarrassed emotion – then he forces himself to a bold decision, pushes open the door, and walks in. He stands there, casts a shy glance at* ANNA, *whose brilliant clothes, and, to him, high-toned appearance awe him terribly. He looks about him with pitiful nervousness as if to avoid the appraising look with which she takes in his face, his clothes, etc. – his voice seeming to plead for her forbearance.*] Anna!

ANNA [*acutely embarrassed in her turn*]: Hallo – father. She told me it was you. I yust got here a little while ago.

CHRIS [*goes slowly over to her chair*]: It's good – for see you – after all dem years, Anna. [*He bends down over her. After an embarrassed struggle they manage to kiss each other.*]

ANNA [*a trace of genuine feeling in her voice*]: It's good to see you, too.

CHRIS [*grasps her arms and looks into her face – then overcome by a wave of fierce tenderness*]: Anna lilla! Anna lilla! [*Takes her in his arms.*]

ANNA [*shrinks away from him, half frightened*]: What's that – Swedish? I don't know it. [*Then as if seeking relief from the tension in a voluble chatter*] Gee, I had an awful trip coming here. I'm all in. I had to sit up in the dirty coach all night – couldn't get no sleep, hardly – and then I had a hard job finding this place. I never been in New York before, you know, and –

CHRIS [*who has been staring down at her face admiringly, not hearing what she says – impulsively*]: You know you vas awful pooty gel, Anna? Ay bet all men see you fall in love with you, py yiminy!

ANNA [*repelled – harshly*]: Cut it! You talk same as they all do.

32

CHRIS [*hurt – humbly*]: Ain't no harm for your fader talk dat vay, Anna.

ANNA [*forcing a short laugh*]: No – course not. Only – it's funny to see you and not remember nothing. You're like – a stranger.

CHRIS [*sadly*]: Ay s'pose. Ay never come home only few times ven you vas kit in Sveden. You don't remember dat?

ANNA: No. [*Resentfully*] But why didn't you never come home them days? Why didn't you never come out West to see me?

CHRIS [*slowly*]: Ay tank, after your mo'der die, ven Ay vas avay on voyage, it's better for you you don't never see me! [*He sinks down in the chair opposite her dejectedly – then turns to her – sadly.*] Ay don't know, Anna, vhy Ay never come home Sveden in ole year. Ay vant come home end of every voyage. Ay vant see your mo'der, your two bro'der before dey vas drowned, you ven you vas born – but – Ay – don't go. Ay sign on oder ships – go South America, go Australia, go China, go every port all over world many times – but Ay never go aboard ship sail for Sveden. Ven Ay gat money for pay passage home as passenger den – [*He bows his head guiltily.*] Ay forgat and Ay spend all money. Ven Ay tank again, it's too late. [*He sighs.*] Ay don't know vhy, but dat's vay with most sailor fallar, Anna. Dat ole davil sea make dem crazy fools with her dirty tricks. It's so.

ANNA [*who has watched him keenly while he has been speaking – with a trace of scorn in her voice*]: Then you think the sea's to blame for everything, eh? Well, you're still workin' on it, ain't you, spite of all you used to write me about hating it. That dame was here told me you was captain of a coal barge – and you wrote me you was yanitor of a building!

CHRIS [*embarrassed but lying glibly*]: Oh, Ay work on land long time as yanitor. Yust short time ago Ay got dis yob cause Ay was sick, need open air.

ANNA [*sceptically*]: Sick? You? You'd never think it.

CHRIS: And, Anna, dis ain't real sailor yob. Dis ain't real boat on sea. She's yust ole tub – like piece of land with house on it dat float. Yob on her ain't sea yob. No. Ay don't gat yob on sea, Anna, if Ay die first. Ay swear dat, ven your mo'der die. Ay keep my word, py yingo!

ANNA [*perplexed*]: Well, I can't see no difference. [*Dismissing the subject*] Speaking of being sick, I been there myself – yust out of the hospital two weeks ago.

CHRIS [*immediately all concern*]: You, Anna? Py golly! [*Anxiously*] You feel better now, dough, don't you? You look little tired, dat's all!

ANNA [*wearily*]: I am. Tired to death. I need a long rest and I don't see much chance of getting it.

CHRIS: What you mean, Anna?

ANNA: Well, when I made up my mind to come to see you, I thought you was a yanitor – that you'd have a place where, maybe, if you didn't mind having me, I could visit a while and rest up – till I felt able to get back on the job again.

CHRIS [*eagerly*]: But Ay gat place, Anna – nice place. You rest all you want, py yiminy! You don't never have to vork as nurse gel no more. You stay with me, py golly!

ANNA [*surprised and pleased by his eagerness – with a smile*]: Then you're really glad to see me – honest?

CHRIS [*pressing one of her hands in both of his*]: Anna, Ay like see you like hell, Ay tal you! And don't you talk no more about gatting yob. You stay with me. Ay don't see you for long time, you don't forgat dat. [*His voice trembles.*] Ay'm gatting ole. Ay gat no one in vorld but you.

ANNA [*touched – embarrassed by this unfamiliar emotion*]: Thanks. It sounds good to hear some one – talk to me that way. Say, though – if you're so lonely – it's funny – why ain't you ever married again?

CHRIS [*shaking his head emphatically – after a pause*]: Ay love your mo'der too much for ever do dat, Anna.

ANNA [*impressed – slowly*]: I don't remember nothing about her. What was she like? Tell me.

CHRIS: Ay tal you all about everytang – and you tal me all tangs happen to you. But not here now. Dis ain't good place for young gel, anyway. Only no good sailor fallar come here for gat drunk. [*He gets to his feet quickly and picks up her bag.*] You come with me, Anna. You need lie down, gat rest.

ANNA [*half-rises to her feet, then sits down again*]: Where're you going?

CHRIS: Come. Ve gat on board.

ANNA [*disappointedly*]: On board your barge, you mean? [*Dryly*] Nix for mine! [*Then seeing his crestfallen look – forcing a smile*] Do you think that's a good place for a young girl like me – a coal barge?

CHRIS [*dully*]: Yes, Ay tank. [*He hesitates – then continues more and more pleadingly.*] You don't know how nice it's on barge, Anna. Tug come and ve gat towed out on voyage – yust water all round, and sun, and fresh air, and good grub for make you strong, healthy gel. You see many tangs you don't see before. You gat moonlight at night, maybe; see steamer pass; see schooner make sail – see everytang dat's pooty. You need take rest like dat. You work too hard for young gel already. You need vacation, yes!

ANNA [*who has listened to him with a growing interest – with an uncertain laugh*]: It sounds good to hear you tell it. I'd sure like a trip on the water, all right. It's the barge idea has me stopped. Well, I'll go down with you and have a look – and maybe I'll take a chance. Gee, I'd do anything once.

CHRIS [*picks up her bag again*]: Ve go, eh?

ANNA: What's the rush? Wait a second. [*Forgetting the situation for a moment, she relapses into the familiar form and flashes one of her winning trade smiles at him.*] Gee, I'm thirsty.

CHRIS [*sets down her bag immediately – hastily*]: Ay'm sorry, Anna. What you tank you like for drink, eh?

ANNA [*promptly*]: I'll take a – [*Then suddenly reminded – confusedly*] I don't know. What's they got here?

CHRIS [*with a grin*]: Ay don't tank dey got much fancy drink for young gel in dis place, Anna. Yinger ale – sas'prilla, maybe.

ANNA [*forcing a laugh herself*]: Make it sas, then.

CHRIS [*coming up to her – with a wink*]: Ay tal you, Anna, ve calabrate, yes – dis one time because ve meet after many year. [*In a half-whisper, embarrassedly*] Dey gat good port vine, Anna. It's good for you, Ay tank – little bit – for give you appetite. It ain't strong, neider. One glass don't go to your head, Ay promise.

ANNA [*with a half-hysterical laugh*]: All right. I'll take port.

CHRIS: Ay go gat him. [*He goes out to the bar. As soon as the door closes,* ANNA *starts to her feet.*]

ANNA [*picking up her bag – half-aloud – stammeringly*]: Gawd, I can't stand this! I better beat it. [*Then she lets her bag drop, stumbles over to her chair again, and covering her face with her hands, begins to sob.*]

LARRY [*putting down his paper as* CHRIS *comes up – with a grin*]: Well, who's the blonde?

CHRIS [*proudly*]: Dat vas Anna, Larry.

LARRY [*in amazement*]: Your daughter, Anna?
[CHRIS *nods.* LARRY *lets a long, low whistle escape him and turns away embarrassedly.*]

CHRIS: Don't you tank she vas pooty gel, Larry?

LARRY [*rising to the occasion*]: Sure! A peach!

CHRIS: You bet you! Give me drink for take back – one port vine for Anna – she calabrate dis one time with me – and small beer for me.

LARRY [*as he gets the drinks*]: Small beer for you, eh? She's reformin' you already.

CHRIS [*pleased*]: You bet! [*He takes the drinks. As she hears him coming,* ANNA *hastily dries her eyes, tries to smile.* CHRIS *comes in and sets the drinks down on the table – stares at her for a second*] *anxiously – patting her hand.*] You look tired, Anna. Vell, Ay make you take good long rest now. [*Picking up his beer*] Come, you drink vine. It put new life in you. [*She lifts her glass – he grins.*] Skoal, Anna! You know dat Svedish word?

ANNA: Skoal! [*Downing her port at a gulp like a drink of whisky – her lips trembling*] Skoal? Guess I know that word, all right, all right!

THE CURTAIN FALLS

ACT TWO

Ten days later. The stern of the deeply laden barge, Simeon
Winthrop, *at anchor in the outer harbour of Provincetown, Mass.
It is ten o'clock at night. Dense fog shrouds the barge on all sides,
and she floats motionless on a calm. A lantern set up on an immense
coil of thick hawser sheds a dull, filtering light on objects near it –
the heavy steel bits for making fast the tow-lines, etc. In the rear is
the cabin, its misty windows glowing wanly with the light of a
lamp inside. The chimney of the cabin stove rises a few feet above
the roof. The doleful tolling of bells, on Long Point, on ships at
anchor, breaks the silence at regular intervals.*

> [*As the curtain rises,* ANNA *is discovered standing near the
> coil of rope on which the lantern is placed. She looks healthy,
> transformed, the natural colour has come back to her face. She
> has on a black, oilskin coat, but wears no hat. She is staring
> out into the fog astern with an expression of awed wonder. The
> cabin door is pushed open and* CHRIS *appears. He is dressed in
> yellow oilskins – coat, trousers, sou'wester –and wears high
> sea-boots.*]

CHRIS [*the glare from the cabin still in his eyes, peers blinkingly
astern*]: Anna! [*Receiving no reply, he calls again, this time with
apparent apprehension.*] Anna!
ANNA [*with a start – making a gesture with her hand as if to
impose silence – in a hushed whisper*]: Yes, here I am. What
d'you want?
CHRIS [*walks over to her – solicitously*]: Don't you come turn
in, Anna? It's late – after four bells. It ain't good for you stay
out here in fog, Ay tank.
ANNA: Why not? [*With a trace of strange exultation*] I love this
fog! Honest! It's so – [*she hesitates, groping for a word*] –
funny and still. I feel as if I was – out of things altogether.

38

CHRIS [*spitting disgustedly*]: Fog's vorst one of her dirty tricks, py yingo!

ANNA [*with a short laugh*]: Beefing about the sea again? I'm getting so's I love it, the little I've seen.

CHRIS [*glancing at her moodily*]: Dat's foolish talk, Anna. You see her more, you don't talk dat vay. [*Then seeing her irritation, he hastily adopts a more cheerful tone.*] But Ay'm glad you like it on barge. Ay'm glad it makes you feel good again. [*With a placating grin*] You like live like dis alone with ole fa'der, eh?

ANNA: Sure I do. Everything's been so different from anything I ever come across before. And now – this fog – Gee, I wouldn't have missed it for nothing. I never thought living on ships was so different from land. Gee, I'd yust love to work on it, honest I would, if I was a man. I don't wonder you always been a sailor.

CHRIS [*vehemently*]: Ay ain't sailor, Anna. And dis ain't real sea. You only see nice part. [*Then as she doesn't answer, he continues hopefully.*] Vell, fog lift in morning, Ay tank.

ANNA [*the exultation again in her voice*]: I love it! I don't give a rap if it never lifts! [CHRIS *fidgets from one foot to the other worriedly.* ANNA *continues slowly, after a pause.*] It makes me feel clean – out here – 's if I'd taken a bath.

CHRIS [*after a pause*]: You better go in cabin – read book. Dat put you to sleep.

ANNA: I don't want to sleep. I want to stay out here – and think about things.

CHRIS [*walks away from her toward the cabin – then comes back*]: You act funny tonight, Anna.

ANNA [*her voice rising angrily*]: Say, what're you trying to do – make things rotten? You been kind as kind can be to me and I certainly appreciate it – only don't spoil it all now. [*Then, seeing the hurt expression on her father's face, she forces a smile.*] Let's talk of something else. Come. Sit down here. [*She points to the coil of rope.*]

CHRIS [*sits down beside her with a sigh*]: It's gatting pooty late in night, Anna. Must be near five bells.

ANNA [*interestedly*]: Five bells? What time is that?

CHRIS: Half past ten.

ANNA: Funny I don't know nothing about sea talk – but those cousins was always talking crops and that stuff. Gee, wasn't I sick of it – and of them!

CHRIS: You don't like live on farm, Anna?

ANNA: I've told you a hundred times I hated it. [*Decidedly*] I'd rather have one drop of ocean than all the farms in the world! Honest! And you wouldn't like a farm, neither. Here's where you belong. [*She makes a sweeping gesture seaward.*] But not on a coal barge. You belong on a real ship, sailing all over the world.

CHRIS [*moodily*]: Ay've done dat many year, Anna, when Ay vas damn fool.

ANNA [*disgustedly*]: Oh, rats! [*After a pause she speaks musingly.*] Was the men in our family always sailors – as far back as you know about?

CHRIS [*shortly*]: Yes. Damn fools! All men in our village on coast, Sveden, go to sea. Ain't nutting else for dem to do. My fa'der die on board ship in Indian Ocean. He's buried at sea. Ay don't never know him only little bit. Den my tree bro'der, older'n me, dey go on ships. Den Ay go, too. Den my mo'der she's left all 'lone. She die pooty quick after dat – all 'lone. Ve vas all avay on voyage when she die. [*He pauses sadly.*] Two my bro'der dey gat lost on fishing boat same like your bro'ders vas drowned. My oder bro'der, he save money, give up sea, den he die home in bed. He's only one dat ole davil don't kill. [*Defiantly*] But me, Ay bet you Ay die ashore in bed, too!

ANNA: Were all of 'em yust plain sailors?

CHRIS: Able body seaman, most of dem. [*With a certain pride*] Dey vas all smart seaman, too – A1. [*Then after hesitating a moment – shyly*] Ay was bos'n.

ANNA: Bos'n?

CHRIS: Dat's kind of officer.

ANNA: Gee, that was fine. What does he do?

CHRIS [*after a second's hesitation, plunged into gloom again by his fear of her enthusiasm*]: Hard vork all time. It's rotten, Ay tal you, for go to sea. [*Determined to disgust her with sea life – volubly*] Dey're all fool fallar, dem fallar in our family. Dey all vork rotten yob on sea for nutting, don't care nutting but yust gat big pay-day in pocket, gat drunk, gat robbed, ship avay again on oder voyage. Dey don't come home. Dey don't do anytang like good man do. And dat ole davil, sea, sooner, later she svallow dem up.

ANNA [*with an excited laugh*]: Good sports, I'd call 'em. [*Then hastily*] But say – listen – did all the women of the family marry sailors?

CHRIS [*eagerly – seeing a chance to drive home his point*]: Yes – and it's bad on dem like hell vorst of all. Dey don't see deir men only once in long while. Dey set and vait all 'lone. And vhen deir boys grows up, go to sea, dey sit and vait some more. [*Vehemently*] Any gel marry sailor, she's crazy fool! Your mo'der she tal you same tang if she vas alive. [*He relapses into an attitude of sombre brooding.*]

ANNA [*after a pause – dreamily*]: Funny! I do feel sort of – nutty, tonight. I feel old.

CHRIS [*mystified*]: Ole?

ANNA: Sure – like I'd been living a long, long time – out here in the fog. [*Frowning perplexedly*] I don't know how to tell you yust what I mean. It's like I'd come home after a long visit away some place. It all seems like I'd been here before lots of times – on boats – in this same fog. [*With a short laugh*] You must think I'm off my base.

CHRIS [*gruffly*]: Anybody feel funny dat vay in fog.

ANNA [*persistently*]: But why d'you s'pose I feel so – so – like I'd found something I'd missed and been looking for – 's if this was the right place for me to fit in? And I seem to have forgot – everything that's happened – like it didn't matter no more. And I feel clean, somehow – like you feel yust after you've took a bath. And I feel happy for once – yes, honest! – happier than I ever been anywhere before! [*As* CHRIS *makes no comment but a heavy sigh, she continues wonderingly.*] It's nutty for me to feel that way, don't you think?

CHRIS [*a grim foreboding in his voice*]: Ay tank Ay'm damn fool for bring you on voyage, Anna.

ANNA [*impressed by his tone*]: You talk – nutty tonight yourself. You act's if you was scared something was going to happen.

CHRIS: Only God know dat, Anna.

ANNA [*half-mockingly*]: Then it'll be Gawd's will, like the preachers say – what does happen.

CHRIS [*starts to his feet with fierce protest*]: No! Dat ole davil, sea, she ain't God! [*In the pause of silence that comes after his defiance a hail in a man's husky, exhausted voice comes faintly out of the fog to port.* 'Ahoy!' CHRIS *gives a startled exclamation.*]

ANNA [*jumping to her feet*]: What's that?

CHRIS [*who has regained his composure – sheepishly*]: Py golly, dat scare me for minute. It's only some fallar hail, Anna – loose his course in fog. Must be fisherman's power boat. His engine break down, Ay guess. [*The* 'Ahoy' *comes again through the wall of fog, sounding much nearer this time.* CHRIS *goes over to the port bulwark.*] Sound from dis side. She come in from open sea. [*He holds his hands to his mouth, megaphone-fashion, and shouts back.*] Ahoy, dere! Vhat's trouble?

THE VOICE [*this time sounding nearer but up forward toward the bow*]: Heave a rope when we come alongside. [*Then irritably*] Where are ye, ye scut?

CHRIS: Ay hear dem rowing. Dey come up by bow, Ay tank [*Then shouting out again*] Dis vay!

THE VOICE: Right ye are! [*There is a muffled sound of oars in rowlocks.*]

ANNA [*half to herself – resentfully*]: Why don't that guy stay where he belongs?

CHRIS [*hurriedly*]: Ay go up bow. All hands asleep 'cepting fallar on vatch. Ay gat heave line to dat fallar. [*He picks up a coil of rope and hurries off toward the bow.* ANNA *walks back toward the extreme stern as if she wanted to remain as much isolated as possible. She turns her back on the proceedings and stares out into the fog.* THE VOICE *is heard again shouting* 'Ahoy' *and* CHRIS *answering* 'Dis vay.' *Then there is a pause – the murmur of excited voices – then the scuffling of feet.* CHRIS *appears from around the cabin to port. He is supporting the limp form of a man dressed in dungarees, holding one of the man's arms around his neck. The deckhand,* JOHNSON, *a young, blond Swede, follows him, helping along another exhausted man similar fashion.* ANNA *turns to look at them.* CHRIS *stops for a second – volubly*] Anna! You come help, vill you? You find vhisky in cabin. Dese fallars need drink for fix dem. Dey vas near dead.

ANNA [*hurrying to him*]: Sure – but who are they? What's the trouble?

CHRIS: Sailor fallars. Deir steamer gat wrecked. Dey been five days in open boat – four fallars – only one left able stand up. Come, Anna. [*She precedes him into the cabin, holding the door open while he and* JOHNSON *carry in their burdens. The door is shut, then opened again as* JOHNSON *comes out.* CHRIS'S *voice shouts after him.*] Go gat oder fallar, Yohnson.

JOHNSON: Yes, sir.

[*He goes. The door is closed again.* MAT BURKE *stumbles in around the port side of the cabin. He moves slowly, feeling his way uncertainly, keeping hold of the port bulwark with his right hand to steady himself. He is stripped to the waist, has on nothing but a pair of dirty dungaree trousers. He is a powerful, broad-chested six-footer, his face handsome in a hard, rough, bold, defiant way. He is about thirty, in the full power of his heavy-muscled, immense strength. His dark eyes are bloodshot and wild from sleeplessness. The muscles of his arms*

43

and shoulders are lumped in knots and bunches, the veins of his forearms stand out like blue cords. He finds his way to the coil of hawser and sits down on it facing the cabin, his back bowed, head in his hands in an attitude of spent weariness.]

BURKE [*talking aloud to himself*]: Row, ye divil! Row! [*Then lifting his head and looking about him*] What's this tub? Well, we're safe, anyway – with the help of God. [*He makes the sign of the cross mechanically.* JOHNSON *comes along the deck to port, supporting the fourth man, who is babbling to himself incoherently.* BURKE *glances at him disdainfully.*] Is it losing the small wits ye iver had, ye are? Deck-scrubbing scut! [*They pass him and go into the cabin, leaving the door open.* BURKE *sags forward wearily.*] I'm bate out – bate out entirely.

ANNA [*comes out of the cabin with a tumbler quarter-full of whisky in her hand. She gives a start when she sees* BURKE *so near her, the light from the open door falling full on him. Then, overcoming what is evidently a feeling of repulsion, she comes up beside him*]: Here you are. Here's a drink for you. You need it, I guess.

BURKE [*lifting his head slowly – confusedly*]: Is it dreaming I am?

ANNA [*half-smiling*]: Drink it and you'll find it ain't no dream.

BURKE: To hell with the drink – but I'll take it just the same. [*He tosses it down.*] Aah! I'm needin' that – and 'tis fine stuff. [*Looking up at her with frank, grinning admiration*] But 'twasn't the booze I meant when I said, was I dreaming. I thought you was some mermaid out of the sea come to torment me. [*He reaches out to feel her arm.*] Aye, rale flesh and blood, divil a less.

ANNA [*coldly. Stepping back from him*]: Cut that.

BURKE: But tell me, isn't this a barge I'm on – or isn't it?

ANNA: Sure.

BURKE: And what is a fine, handsome woman the like of you doing on this scow?

ANNA [*coldly*]: Never you mind. [*Then half-amused in spite of herself*] Say, you're a great one, honest – starting right in kidding after what you been through.

BURKE [*delighted –proudly*]: Ah, it was nothing – aisy for a rale man with guts to him, the like of me. [*He laughs.*] All in the day's work, darlin'. [*Then, more seriously, but still in a boastful tone, confidentially*] But I won't be denying 'twas a damn narrow squeak. We'd all ought to be with Davy Jones at the bottom of the sea, be rights. And only for me, I'm telling you, and the great strength and guts is in me, we'd be being scoffed by the fishes this minute!

ANNA [*contemptuously*]: Gee, you hate yourself, don't you? [*Then turning away from him indifferently*] Well, you'd better come in and lie down. You must want to sleep.

BURKE [*stung – rising unsteadily to his feet with chest out and head thrown back – resentfully*]: Lie down and sleep, is it? Divil a wink I'm after having for two days and nights and divil a bit I'm needing now. Let you not be thinking I'm the like of them three weak scuts come in the boat with me. I could lick the three of them sitting down with one hand tied behind me. They may be bate out, but I'm not – and I've been rowing the boat with them lying in the bottom not able to raise a hand for the last two days we was in it. [*Furiously, as he sees this is making no impression on her*] And I can lick all hands on this tub, wan be wan, tired as I am!

ANNA [*sarcastically*]: Gee, ain't you a hard guy! [*Then, with a trace of sympathy, as she notices him swaying from weakness*] But never mind that fight talk. I'll take your word for all you've said. Go on and sit down out here, anyway, if I can't get you to come inside. [*He sits down weakly.*] You're all in, you might as well own up to it.

BURKE [*fiercely*]: The hell I am!

ANNA [*coldly*]: Well, be stubborn then for all I care. And I must say I don't care for your language. The men I know don't pull that rough stuff when ladies are around.

BURKE [*getting unsteadily to his feet again – in a rage*]: Ladies!

Ho-ho! Divil mend you! Let you not be making game of me. What would ladies be doing on this bloody hulk? [*As* ANNA *attempts to go to the cabin, he lurches into her path.*] Aisy, now! You're not the old Square-head's woman, I suppose you'll be telling me next – living in his cabin with him, no less! [*Seeing the cold, hostile expression on* ANNA'S *face, he suddenly changes his tone to one of boisterous joviality.*] But I do be thinking, iver since the first look my eyes took at you, that it's a fool you are to be wasting yourself – a fine, handsome girl – on a stumpy runt of a man like that old Swede. There's too many strapping great lads on the sea would give their heart's blood for one kiss of you!

ANNA [*scornfully*]: Lads like you, eh?

BURKE [*grinning*]: Ye take the words out o' my mouth. I'm the proper lad for you, if it's meself do be saying it. [*With a quick movement he puts his arms about her waist.*] Whisht, now, me daisy! Himself's in the cabin. It's wan of your kisses I'm needing to take the tiredness from me bones. Wan kiss, now! [*He presses her to him and attempts to kiss her.*]

ANNA [*struggling fiercely*]: Leggo of me, you big mut!

[*She pushes him away with all her might.* BURKE, *weak and tottering, is caught off his guard. He is thrown down backward, and, in falling, hits his head a hard thump against the bulwark. He lies there still, knocked out for the moment.* ANNA *stands for a second, looking down at him anxiously. Then she kneels down beside him and raises his head to her knee, staring into his face for some sign of life.*]

BURKE [*stirring a bit – mutteringly*]: God stiffen it! [*He opens his eyes and blinks up at her with vague wonder.*]

ANNA [*letting his head sink back on the deck, rising to her feet with a sigh of relief*]: You're coming to all right, eh? Gee, I was scared for a moment I'd killed you.

BURKE [*with difficulty rising to a sitting position – scornfully*]: Killed, is it? It'd take more than a bit of a blow to crack my thick skull. [*Then looking at her with the most intense admira-*

46

tion] But, glory be, it's a power of strength is in them two fine arms of yours. There's not a man in the world can say the same as you, that he seen Mat Burke lying at his feet and him dead to the world.

ANNA [*rather remorsefully*]: Forget it. I'm sorry it happened, see? [BURKE *rises and sits on bench. Then severely*] Only you had no right to be getting fresh with me. Listen, now, and don't go getting any more wrong notions. I'm on this barge because I'm making a trip with my father. The captain's my father. Now you know.

BURKE: The old square – the old Swede, I mean?

ANNA: Yes.

BURKE [*rising – peering at her face*]: Sure, I might have known it, if I wasn't a bloody fool from birth. Where else'd you get that fine yellow hair is like a golden crown on your head.

ANNA [*with an amused laugh*]: Say, nothing stops you, does it? [*Then attempting a severe tone again*] But don't you think you ought to be apologizing for what you said and done yust a minute ago, instead of trying to kid me with that mush?

BURKE [*indignantly*]: Mush! [*Then bending forward toward her with very intense earnestness*] Indade, and I will ask your pardon a thousand times – and on my knees, if ye like. I didn't mean a word of what I said or did. [*Resentful again for a second*] But divil a woman in all the ports of the world has iver made a great fool of me that way before!

ANNA [*with amused sarcasm*]: I see. You mean you're a lady-killer and they all fall for you.

BURKE [*offended. Passionately*]: Leave off your fooling! 'Tis that is after getting my back up at you. [*Earnestly*] 'Tis no lie I'm telling you about the women. [*Ruefully*] Though it's a great jackass I am to be mistaking you, even in anger, for the like of them cows on the water-front is the only women I've met up with since I was growed to a man. [*As ANNA shrinks away from him at this, he hurries on pleadingly.*] I'm a hard, rough man, and I'm not fit, I'm thinking, to be kissing

the shoe-soles of a fine, dacent girl the like of yourself. 'Tis
only the ignorance of your kind made me see you wrong.
So you'll forgive me, for the love of God, and let us be
friends from this out. [*Passionately*] I'm thinking I'd rather
be friends with you than have my wish for anything else
in the world. [*He holds out his hand to her shyly.*]

ANNA [*looking queerly at him, perplexed and worried, but moved
and pleased in spite of herself – takes his hand uncertainly*]: Sure.

BURKE [*with boyish delight*]: God bless you! [*In his excitement
he squeezes her hand tight.*]

ANNA: Ouch!

BURKE [*hastily dropping her hand – ruefully*]: Your pardon,
Miss. 'Tis a clumsy ape I am. [*Then simply – glancing down his
arm proudly*] It's great power I have in my hand and arm,
and I do be forgetting it at times.

ANNA [*nursing her crushed hand and glancing at his arm, not
without a trace of his own admiration*]: Gee, you're some strong,
all right.

BURKE [*delighted*]: It's no lie, and why shouldn't I be, with me
shovelling a million tons of coal in the stokeholes of ships
since I was a lad only. [*He pats the coil of hawser invitingly.*]
Let you sit down, now, Miss, and I'll be telling you a bit of
myself, and you'll be telling me a bit of yourself, and in an
hour we'll be as old friends as if we was born in the same
house. [*He pulls at her sleeve shyly.*] Sit down now, if you
plaze.

ANNA [*with a half-laugh*]: Well – [*She sits down.*] But we won't
talk about me, see? You tell me about yourself and about
the wreck.

BURKE [*flattered*]: I'll tell you, surely. But can I be asking you
one question, Miss, has my head in a puzzle?

ANNA [*guardedly*]: Well – I dunno – what is it?

BURKE: What is it you do when you're not taking a trip with
the Old Man? For I'm thinking a fine girl the like of you
ain't living always on this tub.

ANNA [*uneasily*]: No – of course I ain't. [*She searches his face suspiciously, afraid there may be some hidden insinuation in his words. Seeing his simple frankness, she goes on confidently.*] Well, I'll tell you. I'm a governess, see? I take care of kids for people and learn them things.

BURKE [*impressed*]: A governess, is it? You must be smart, surely.

ANNA: But let's not talk about me. Tell me about the wreck, like you promised me you would.

BURKE [*importantly*]: 'Twas this way, Miss. Two weeks out we ran into the divil's own storm, and she sprang wan hell of a leak up for'ard. The skipper was hoping to make Boston before another blow would finish her, but ten days back we met up with another storm the like of the first, only worse. Four days we was in it with green seas raking over her from bow to stern. That was a terrible time, God help us. [*Proudly*] And if 'twasn't for me and my great strength, I'm telling you – and it's God's truth – there'd been mutiny itself in the stokehole. 'Twas me held them to it, with a kick to wan and a clout to another, and they not caring a damn for the engineers any more, but fearing a clout of my right arm more than they'd fear the sea itself. [*He glances at her anxiously, eager for her approval.*]

ANNA [*concealing a smile – amused by this boyish boasting of his*]: You did some hard work, didn't you?

BURKE [*promptly*]: I did that! I'm a divil for sticking it out when them that's weak give up. But much good it did anyone! 'Twas a mad, fightin' scramble in the last seconds with each man for himself. I disremember how it come about, but there was the four of us in wan boat, and when we was raised high on a great wave I took a look about and divil a sight there was of ship or men on top of the sea.

ANNA [*in a subdued voice*]: Then all the others was drowned?

BURKE: They was, surely.

ANNA [*with a shudder*]: What a terrible end!

BURKE [*turns to her*]: A terrible end for the like of them swabs does live on land, maybe. But for the like of us does be roaming the seas, a good end, I'm telling you – quick and clane.

ANNA [*struck by the word*]: Yes, clean. That's yust the word for – all of it – the way it makes me feel.

BURKE: The sea, you mean? [*Interestedly*] I'm thinking you have a bit of it in your blood, too. Your Old Man wasn't only a barge rat – begging your pardon – all his life, by the cut of him.

ANNA: No, he was bo'sun on sailing ships for years. And all the men on both sides of the family have gone to sea as far back as he remembers, he says. All the women have married sailors, too.

BURKE [*with intense satisfaction*]: Did they, now? They had spirit in them. It's only on the sea you'd find rale men with guts is fit to wed with fine, high-tempered girls – [*then he adds half-boldly*] – the like of yourself.

ANNA [*with a laugh*]: There you go kiddin' again. [*Then seeing his hurt expression – quickly*] But you was going to tell me about yourself. You're Irish, of course I can tell that.

BURKE [*stoutly*]: Yes, thank God, though I've not seen a sight of it in fifteen years or more.

ANNA [*thoughtfully*]: Sailors never do go home hardly, do they? That's what my father was saying.

BURKE: He wasn't telling no lie. [*With sudden melancholy*] It's a hard and lonesome life, the sea is. The only women you'd meet in the ports of the world who'd be willing to speak you a kind word isn't women at all. You know the kind I mane, and they're a poor, wicked lot, God forgive them. They're looking to steal the money from you only.

ANNA [*her face averted – rising to her feet – agitatedly*]: I think – I guess I'd better see what's doing inside.

BURKE [*afraid he has offended her – beseechingly*]: Don't go, I'm saying! Is it I've given you offence with my talk of the like of them? Don't heed it at all! I'm clumsy in my wits when it comes to talking proper with a girl the like of you. And why wouldn't I be? Since the day I left home for to go to sea punching coal, this is the first time I've had a word with a rale, dacent woman. So don't turn your back on me now, and we beginning to be friends.

ANNA [*turning to him again – forcing a smile*]: I'm not sore at you, honest.

BURKE [*gratefully*]: God bless you!

ANNA [*changing the subject abruptly*]: But if you honestly think the sea's such a rotten life, why don't you get out of it?

BURKE [*surprised*]: Work on land, is it? [*She nods. He spits scornfully.*] Digging spuds in the muck from dawn to dark, I suppose? [*Vehemently*] I wasn't made for it, Miss.

ANNA [*with a laugh*]: I thought you'd say that.

BURKE [*argumentatively*]: But there's good jobs and bad jobs at sea, like there'd be on land. I'm thinking if it's in the stokehole of a proper liner I was, I'd be able to have a little house and be home to it wan week out of four. And I'm thinking that maybe then I'd have the luck to find a fine dacent girl – the like of yourself, now – would be willing to wed with me.

ANNA [*turning away from him with a short laugh – uneasily*]: Why, sure. Why not?

BURKE [*edging up close to her – exultantly*]: Then you think a girl the like of yourself might maybe not mind the past at all but only be seeing the good herself put in me?

ANNA [*in the same tone*]: Why, sure.

BURKE [*passionately*]: She'd not be sorry for it, I'd take my oath! 'Tis no more drinking and roving about I'd be doing then, but giving my pay-day into her hand and staying at home with her as meek as a lamb each night of the week I'd be in port.

ANNA [*moved in spite of herself and troubled by this half-concealed proposal – with a forced laugh*]: All you got to do is find the girl.

BURKE: I have found her!

ANNA [*half-frightened – trying to laugh it off*]: You have? When? I thought you was saying –

BURKE [*boldly and forcefully*]: This night. [*Hanging his head – humbly*] If she'll be having me. [*Then raising his eyes to hers – simply*] 'Tis you I mean.

ANNA [*is held by his eyes for a moment – then shrinks back from him with a strange, broken laugh*]: Say – are you – going crazy? Are you trying to kid me? Proposing – to me! – for Gawd's sake! – on such short acquaintance?

    CHRIS *comes out of the cabin and stands staring blinkingly astern. When he makes out* ANNA *in such intimate proximity to this strange sailor, an angry expression comes over his face.*]

BURKE [*following her – with fierce, pleading insistence*]: I'm telling you there's the will of God in it that brought me safe through the storm and fog to the wan spot in the world where you was! Think of that now, and isn't it queer –

CHRIS: Anna! [*He comes toward them, raging, his fists clenched.*] Anna, you gat in cabin, you hear!

ANNA [*all her emotions immediately transformed into resentment at his bullying tone*]: Who d'you think you're talking to – a slave?

CHRIS [*hurt – his voice breaking – pleadingly*]: You need gat rest, Anna. You gat sleep. [*She does not move. He turns on* BURKE *furiously.*] What you doing here, you sailor fallar? You ain't sick like oders. You gat in fo'c'sle. Dey give you bunk. [*Threateningly*] You hurry, Ay tal you!

ANNA [*impulsively*]: But he is sick. Look at him. He can hardly stand up.

BURKE [*straightening and throwing out his chest – with a bold laugh*]: Is it giving me orders ye are, me bucko? Let you look out, then! With wan hand, weak as I am, I can break ye in two and fling the pieces over the side – and your crew after you. [*Stopping abruptly*] I was forgetting. You're her Old Man, and I'd not raise a fist to you for the world.

[*His knees sag, he wavers and seems about to fall.* ANNA *utters an exclamation of alarm and hurries to his side.*]

ANNA [*taking one of his arms over her shoulder*]: Come on in the cabin. You can have my bed if there ain't no other place.

BURKE [*with jubilant happiness – as they proceed toward the cabin*]: Glory be to God, is it holding my arm about your neck you are! Anna! Anna! Sure, it's a sweet name is suited to you.

ANNA [*guiding him carefully*]: Sssh! Sssh!

BURKE: Whisht, is it? Indade, and I'll not. I'll be roaring it out like a fog horn over the sea! You're the girl of the world, and we'll be marrying soon, and I don't care who knows it!

ANNA [*as she guides him through the cabin door*]: Ssshh! Never mind that talk. You go to sleep.

They go out of sight in the cabin. CHRIS, *who has been listening to* BURKE'S *last words with open-mouthed amazement, stands looking after them helplessly.*]

CHRIS [*turns suddenly and shakes his fist out at the sea – with bitter hatred*]: Dat's your dirty trick, damn ole davil, you! [*Then in a frenzy of rage*] But, py God, you don't do dat! Not while Ay'm living! No, py God, you don't!

THE CURTAIN FALLS

ACT THREE

The interior of the cabin on the barge, Simeon Winthrop (*at dock in Boston*) — *a narrow, low-ceilinged compartment, the walls of which are painted a light brown with white trimmings. In the rear on the left, a door leading to the sleeping quarters. In the far left corner, a large locker-closet, painted white, on the door of which a mirror hangs on a nail. In the rear wall, two small square windows and a door opening out on the deck toward the stern. In the right wall, two more windows looking out on the port deck. White curtains, clean and stiff, are at the windows. A table with two canebottomed chairs stands in the centre of the cabin. A dilapidated, wicker rocker, painted brown, is also by the table.*

It is afternoon of a sunny day about a week later. From the harbour and docks outside, muffled by the closed door and windows, comes the sound of steamers' whistles and the puffing snort of the donkey engines of some ship unloading near by.

> [*As the curtain rises,* CHRIS *and* ANNA *are discovered.* ANNA *is seated in the rocking-chair by the table, with a newspaper in her hands. She is not reading but staring straight in front of her. She looks unhappy, troubled, frowningly concentrated on her thoughts.* CHRIS *wanders about the room, casting quick, uneasy side glances at her face, then stopping to peer absentmindedly out of the window. His attitude betrays an overwhelming, gloomy anxiety which has him on tenterhooks. He pretends to be engaged in setting things shipshape, but this occupation is confined to picking up some object, staring at it stupidly for a second, then aimlessly putting it down again. He clears his throat and starts to sing to himself in a low, doleful voice:* 'My Yosephine, come aboard de ship. Long time Ay vait for you.']

ANNA [*turning on him, sarcastically*]: I'm glad some one's feeling good. [*Wearily*] Gee, I sure wish we was out of this dump and back in New York.

CHRIS [*with a sigh*]: Ay'm glad when ve sail again, too. [*Then, as she makes no comment, he goes on with a ponderous attempt at sarcasm.*] Ay don't see vhy you don't like Boston, dough. You have good time here, Ay tank. You go ashore all time, every day and night veek ve've been here. You go to movies, see show, gat all kinds fun – [*His eyes hard with hatred*] All with that damn Irish fallar!

ANNA [*with weary scorn*]: Oh, for heaven's sake, are you off on that again? Where's the harm in his taking me around? D'you want me to sit all day and night in this cabin with you – and knit? Ain't I got a right to have as good a time as I can?

CHRIS: It ain't right kind of fun – not with that fallar, no.

ANNA: I been back on board every night by eleven, ain't I? [*Then struck by some thought – looks at him with keen suspicion – with rising anger.*] Say, look here, what d'you mean by what you yust said?

CHRIS [*hastily*]: Nutting but what Ay say, Anna.

ANNA: You said 'ain't right' and you said it funny. Say, listen here, you ain't trying to insinuate that there's something wrong between us, are you?

CHRIS [*horrified*]: No, Anna! No, Ay svear to God, Ay never tank dat!

ANNA [*mollified by his very evident sincerity – sitting down again*]: Well, don't you never think it neither if you want me ever to speak to you again. [*Angrily again*] If I ever dreamt you thought that, I'd get the hell out of this barge so quick you couldn't see me for dust.

CHRIS [*soothingly*]: Ay wouldn't never dream – [*Then, after a second's pause, reprovingly*] You vas gatting learn to svear. Dat ain't nice for young gel, you tank?

ANNA [*with a faint trace of a smile*]: Excuse me. You ain't used to such language, I know. [*Mockingly*] That's what your taking me to sea has done for me.

CHRIS [*indignantly*]: No, it ain't me. It's dat damn sailor fallar learn you bad tangs.

ANNA: He ain't a sailor. He's a stoker.

CHRIS [*forcibly*]: Dat vas million times vorse, Ay tal you! Dem fallars dat vork below shovelling coal vas de dirtiest, rough gang of no-good fallars in vorld!

ANNA: I'd hate to hear you say that to Mat.

CHRIS: Oh, Ay tal him same tang. You don't gat it in head Ay'm scared of him yust 'cause he vas stronger'n Ay vas. [*Menacingly*] You don't gat for fight with fists with dem fallars. Dere's oder vay for fix him.

ANNA [*glancing at him with sudden alarm*]: What d'you mean?

CHRIS [*sullenly*]: Nutting.

ANNA: You'd better not. I wouldn't start no trouble with him if I was you. He might forget some time that you was old and my father – and then you'd be out of luck.

CHRIS [*with smouldering hatred*]: Vell, yust let him! Ay'm ole bird maybe, but Ay bet Ay show him trick or two.

ANNA [*suddenly changing her tone – persuasively*]: Aw come on, be good. What's eating you, anyway? Don't you want no one to be nice to me except yourself?

CHRIS [*placated – coming to her – eagerly*]: Yes, Ay do, Anna – only not fallar on sea. But Ay like for you marry steady fallar got good yob on land. You have little home in country all your own –

ANNA [*rising to her feet – brusquely*]: Oh, cut it out! [*Scornfully*] Little home in the country! I wish you could have seen the little home in the country where you had me in jail till I was sixteen! [*With rising irritation*] Some day you're going to get me so mad with that talk, I'm going to turn loose on you and tell you – a lot of things that'll open your eyes.

CHRIS [*alarmed*]: Ay don't vant –

ANNA: I know you don't; but you keep on talking yust the same.

CHRIS: Ay don't talk no more den, Anna.

ANNA: Then promise me you'll cut out saying nasty things about Mat Burke every chance you get.

CHRIS [*evasive and suspicious*]: Vhy? You like dat fallar – very much, Anna?

ANNA: Yes, I certainly do! He's a regular man, no matter what faults he's got. One of his fingers is worth all the hundreds of men I met out there – inland.

CHRIS [*his face darkening*]: Maybe you tank you love him, den?

ANNA [*defiantly*]: What of it if I do.

CHRIS [*scowling and forcing out the words*]: Maybe – you tank you – marry him?

ANNA [*shaking her head*]: No! [CHRIS's *face lights up with relief.* ANNA *continues slowly, a trace of sadness in her voice.*] If I'd met him four years ago – or even two years ago – I'd have jumped at the chance, I tell you that straight. And I would now – only he's such a simple guy – a big kid – and I ain't got the heart to fool him. [*She breaks off suddenly.*] But don't never say again he ain't good enough for me. It's me ain't good enough for him.

CHRIS [*snorts scornfully*]: Py yiminy, you go crazy, Ay tank!

ANNA [*with a mournful laugh*]: Well, I been thinking I was myself the last few days. [*She goes and takes a shawl from a hook near the door and throws it over her shoulders.*] Guess I'll take a walk down to the end of the dock for a minute and see what's doing. I love to watch the ships passing. Mat'll be along before long, I guess. Tell him where I am, will you?

CHRIS [*despondently*]: All right, Ay tal him.

[ANNA *goes out the doorway on rear.* CHRIS *follows her out and stands on the deck outside for a moment looking after her. Then he comes back inside and shuts the door. He stands looking out of the window – mutters –* 'Dirty ole davil, you.' *Then he goes to the table, sets the cloth straight mechanically, picks up the newspaper* ANNA *has let fall to the floor, and sits down in the rocking-chair. He stares at the paper for a while,*

*then puts it on the table, holds his head in his hands, and sighs
drearily. The noise of a man's heavy footsteps comes from the
deck outside and there is a loud knock on the door.* CHRIS
*starts, makes a move as if to get up and go to the door, then
thinks better of it and sits still. The knock is repeated – then as
no answer comes, the door is flung open and* MAT BURKE
appears. CHRIS *scowls at the intruder and his hand instinctively
goes back to the sheath knife on his hip.* BURKE *is dressed up –
wears a cheap blue suit, a striped cotton shirt with a black tie,
and black shoes newly shined. His face is beaming with good
humour.*]

BURKE [*as he sees* CHRIS – *in a jovial tone of mockery*]: Well,
God bless who's here! [*He bends down and squeezes his huge
form through the narrow doorway.*] And how is the world
treating you this afternoon, Anna's father?

CHRIS [*sullenly*]: Pooty goot – if it ain't for some fallars.

BURKE [*with a grin*]: Meaning me, do you? [*He laughs.*] Well,
if you ain't the funny old crank of a man! [*Then soberly*]
Where's herself? [CHRIS *sits dumb, scowling, his eyes averted.*
BURKE *is irritated by this silence.*] Where's Anna, I'm after
asking you?

CHRIS [*hesitating – then grouchily*]: She go down end of dock.

BURKE: I'll be going down to her, then. But first I'm thinking
I'll take this chance when we're alone to have a word with
you. [*He sits down opposite* CHRIS *at the table and leans over
toward him.*] And that word is soon said. I'm marrying
your Anna before this day is out, and you might as well
make up your mind to it whether you like it or no.

CHRIS [*glaring at him with hatred and forcing a scornful laugh*]:
Ho-ho! Dat's easy for say!

BURKE: You mean I won't? [*Scornfully*] Is it the like of yourself will stop me, are you thinking?

CHRIS: Yes, Ay stop it, if it come to vorst.

BURKE [*with scornful pity*]: God help you!

CHRIS: But ain't no need for me do dat. Anna –

BURKE [*smiling confidently*]: Is it Anna you think will prevent me?

CHRIS: Yes.

BURKE: And I'm telling you she'll not. She knows I'm loving her, and she loves me the same, and I know it.

CHRIS: Ho-ho! She only have fun. She make big fool of you, dat's all!

BURKE [*unshaken – pleasantly*]: That's a lie in your throat, divil mend you!

CHRIS: No, it ain't lie. She tal me yust before she go out she never marry fallar like you.

BURKE: I'll not believe it. 'Tis a great old liar you are, and a divil to be making a power of trouble if you had your way. But 'tis not trouble I'm looking for, and me sitting down here. [*Earnestly*] Let us be talking it out now as man to man. You're her father, and wouldn't it be a shame for us to be at each other's throats like a pair of dogs, and I married with Anna. So out with the truth, man alive. What is it you're holding against me at all?

CHRIS [*a bit placated, in spite of himself, by* BURKE'S *evident sincerity – but puzzled and suspicious*]: Vell – Ay don't vant for Anna gat married. Listen, you fallar. Ay'm a ole man. Ay don't see Anna for fifteen year. She vas all Ay gat in vorld. And now ven she come on first trip – you tank Ay vant her leave me 'lone again?

BURKE [*heartily*]: Let you not be thinking I have no heart at all for the way you'd be feeling.

CHRIS [*astonished and encouraged – trying to plead persuasively*]: Den you do right tang, eh? You ship avay again, leave Anna alone. [*Cajolingly*] Big fallar like you dat's on sea, he don't need vife. He gat new gel in every port, you know dat.

BURKE [*angry for a second*]: God stiffen you! [*Then controlling himself – calmly*] I'll not be giving you the lie on that. But divil take you, there's a time comes to every man, on sea or land, that isn't a born fool, when he's sick of the lot of them cows, and wearing his heart out to meet up with a fine dacent girl, and have a home to call his own and be rearing up children in it. 'Tis small use you're asking me to leave Anna. She's the wan woman of the world for me, and I can't live without her now, I'm thinking.

CHRIS: You forgat all about her in one veek out of port, Ay bet you!

BURKE: You don't know the like I am. Death itself wouldn't make me forget her. So let you not be making talk to me about leaving her. I'll not, and be damned to you! It won't be so bad for you as you'd make out at all. She'll be living here in the States, and her married to me. And you'd be seeing her often so – a sight more often than ever you saw her the fifteen years she was growing up in the West. It's quare you'd be the one to be making great trouble about her leaving you when you never laid eyes on her once in all them years.

CHRIS [guiltily]: Ay taught it vas better Anna stay avay, grow up inland where she don't ever know ole davil, sea.

BURKE [scornfully]: Is it blaming the sea for your troubles ye are again, God help you? Well, Anna knows it now. 'Twas in her blood, anyway.

CHRIS: And Ay don't vant she ever know no-good fallar on sea –

BURKE: She knows one now.

CHRIS [banging the table with his fist – furiously]: Dat's yust it! Dat's yust what you are – no-good, sailor fallar! You tank Ay lat her life be made sorry by you like her mo'der's vas by me! No, Ay swear! She don't marry you if Ay gat kill you first!

BURKE [looks at him a moment, in astonishment – then laughing uproariously]: Ho-ho! Glory be to God, it's bold talk you have for a stumpy runt of a man!

CHRIS [threateningly]: Vell – you see!

BURKE [with grinning defiance]: I'll see, surely! I'll see myself and Anna married this day, I'm telling you! [*Then with contemptuous exasperation*]It's quare fool's blather you have about the sea done this and the sea done that. You'd ought to be shamed to be saying the like, and you an old sailor yourself. I'm after hearing a lot of it from you and a lot more that Anna's told me you do be saying to her, and I'm thinking it's a poor weak thing you are, and not a man at all!

CHRIS [*darkly*]: You see if Ay'm man – maybe quicker'n you tank.

BURKE [*contemptuously*]: Yerra, don't be boasting. I'm thinking 'tis out of your wits you've got with fright of the sea. You'd be wishing Anna married to a farmer, she told me. That'd be a swate match, surely. Would you have a fine girl the like of Anna lying down at nights with a muddy scut stinking of pigs and dung? Or would you have her tied for life to the like of them skinny, shrivelled swabs does be working in cities?

CHRIS: Dat's lie, you fool!

BURKE: 'Tis not. 'Tis your own mad notions I'm after telling. But you know the truth in your heart, if great fear of the sea has made you a liar and coward itself. [*Pounding the table*] The sea's the only life for a man with guts in him isn't afraid of his own shadow! 'Tis only on the sea he's free, and him roving the face of the world, seeing all things, and not giving a damn for saving up money, or stealing from his friends, or any of the black tricks that a landlubber'd waste his life on. 'Twas yourself knew it once, and you a bo'sun for years.

CHRIS [*sputtering with rage*]: You vas crazy fool, Ay tal you!

BURKE: You've swallowed the anchor. The sea give you a clout once knocked you down, and you're not man enough to get up for another, but lie there for the rest of your life howling bloody murder. [*Proudly*] Isn't it myself the sea has nearly drowned, and me battered and bate till I was that close to hell I could hear the flames roaring, and never a groan out of me till the sea gave up and it seeing the great strength and guts of a man was in me?

CHRIS [*scornfully*]: Yes, you vas hell of fallar, hear you tal it!

BURKE [*angrily*]: You'll be calling me a liar once too often, me old bucko! Wasn't the whole story of it and my picture itself in the newspapers of Boston a week back? [*Looking* CHRIS *up and down belittlingly*] Sure, I'd like to see you in the best of your youth do the like of what I done in the storm and after. 'Tis a mad lunatic, screeching with fear, you'd be this minute!

CHRIS: Ho-ho! You vas young fool! In ole years when Ay was on windyammer, Ay vas through hundred storms vorse'n dat! Ships vas ships den – and men dat sail on dem vas real men. And now what you gat on steamers? You gat fallars on deck don't know ship from mudscow. [*With a meaning glance at* BURKE] And below deck you gat fallars yust know how for shovel coal – might yust as vell vork on coal vagon ashore!

BURKE [*stung – angrily*]: Is it casting insults at the men in the stokehole ye are, ye old ape? God stiffen you! Wan of them is worth any ten stock-fish-swilling Square-heads ever shipped on a windbag!

CHRIS [*his face working with rage, his hand going back to the sheath-knife on his hip*]: Irish svine, you!

BURKE [*tauntingly*]: Don't ye like the Irish, ye old baboon? 'Tis that you're needing in your family, I'm telling you – an Irishman and a man of the stokehole – to put guts in it so that you'll not be having grandchildren would be fearful cowards and jackasses the like of yourself!

CHRIS [*half-rising from his chair – in a voice choked with rage*]: You look out!

BURKE [*watching him intently – a mocking smile on his lips*]: And it's that you'll be having, no matter what you'll do to prevent; for Anna and me'll be married this day, and no old fool the like of you will stop us when I've made up my mind.

CHRIS [*with a hoarse cry*]: You don't!

[*He throws himself at* BURKE, *knife in hand, knocking his chair over backwards.* BURKE *springs to his feet quickly in time to meet the attack. He laughs with the pure love of battle. The old Swede is like a child in his hands.* BURKE *does not strike or mistreat him in any way, but simply twists his right hand behind his back and forces the knife from his fingers. He throws the knife into a far corner of the room – tauntingly.*]

BURKE: Old men is getting childish shouldn't play with knives. [*Holding the struggling* CHRIS *at arm's length – with a sudden rush of anger, drawing back his fist*] I've half a mind to hit you – a great clout will put sense in your square head. Kape off me now, I'm warning you! [*He gives* CHRIS *a push with the flat of his hand which sends the old Swede staggering back against the cabin wall, where he remains standing, panting heavily, his eyes fixed on* BURKE *with hatred, as if he were only collecting his strength to rush at him again. Warningly*] Now don't be coming at me again, I'm saying, or I'll flatten you on the floor with a blow, if 'tis Anna's father you are itself! I've no patience left for you. [*Then with an amused laugh*] Well, 'tis a bold old man you are just the same, and I'd never think it was in you to come tackling me alone. [*A shadow crosses the cabin windows. Both men start.* ANNA *appears in the doorway.*]

ANNA [*with pleased surprise as she sees* BURKE]: Hallo, Mat. Are you here already? I was down – [*She stops, looking from one to the other, sensing immediately that something has happened.*] What's up? [*Then noticing the overturned chair – in alarm*] How'd that chair get knocked over? [*Turning on* BURKE *reproachfully*] You ain't been fighting with him, Mat – after you promised?

BURKE [*his old self again*]: I've not laid a hand on him, Anna. [*He goes and picks up the chair, then turning on the still-questioning* ANNA *– with a reassuring smile*] Let you not be worried at all. 'Twas only a bit of an argument we was having to pass the time till you'd come.

ANNA: It must have been some argument when you got to throwing chairs. [*She turns on* CHRIS.] Why don't you say something? What was it about?

CHRIS [*relaxing at last – avoiding her eyes – sheepishly*]: Ve vas talking about ships and fallars on sea.

ANNA [*with a relieved smile*]: Oh – the old stuff, eh?

BURKE [*suddenly seeming to come to a bold decision – with a defiant grin at* CHRIS]: He's not after telling you the whole of it. We was arguing about you mostly.

ANNA [*with a frown*]: About me?

BURKE: And we'll be finishing it out right here and now in your presence if you're willing. [*He sits down at the left of table.*]

ANNA [*uncertainly – looking from him to her father*]: Sure. Tell me what it's all about.

CHRIS [*advancing toward the table – protesting to* BURKE]: No! You don't do dat, you! You tal him you don't vant for hear him talk, Anna.

ANNA: But I do. I want this cleared up.

CHRIS [*miserably afraid now*]: Vell, not now, anyvay. You vas going ashore, yes? You ain't got time –

ANNA [*firmly*]: Yes, right here and now. [*She turns to* BURKE.] You tell me, Mat, since he don't want to.

BURKE [*draws a deep breath – then plunges in boldly*]: The whole of it's in a few words only. So's he'd make no mistake, and him hating the sight of me, I told him in his teeth I loved you. [*Passionately*] And that's God truth, Anna, and well you know it!

CHRIS [*scornfully – forcing a laugh*]: Ho-ho! He tal same tang to gel every port he go!

ANNA [*shrinking from her father with repulsion – resentfully*]: Shut up, can't you? [*Then to* BURKE – *feelingly*] I know it's true, Mat. I don't mind what he says.

BURKE [*humbly grateful*]: God bless you!

ANNA: And then what?

BURKE: And then – [*Hesitatingly*] And then I said – [*He looks at her pleadingly.*] I said I was sure – I told him I thought you have a bit of love for me, too. [*Passionately*] Say you do, Anna! Let you not destroy me entirely, for the love of God! [*He grasps both her hands in his two.*]

ANNA [*deeply moved and troubled – forcing a trembling laugh*]: So you told him that, Mat? No wonder he was mad. [*Forcing out the words*] Well, maybe it's true, Mat. Maybe I do. I been thinking and thinking – I didn't want to, Mat, I'll own up to that – I tried to cut it out – but – [*She laughs helplessly.*] I guess I can't help it anyhow. So I guess I do, Mat. [*Then with a sudden joyous defiance*] Sure I do! What's the use of kidding myself different? Sure I love you, Mat!

CHRIS [*with a cry of pain*]: Anna! [*He sits crushed.*]

BURKE [*with a great depth of sincerity in his humble gratitude*]: God be praised!

ANNA [*assertively*]: And I ain't never loved a man in my life before, you can always believe that – no matter what happens.

BURKE [*goes over to her and puts his arms around her*]: Sure I do be believing ivery word you iver said or iver will say. And 'tis you and me will be having a grand, beautiful life together to the end of our days!

[*He tries to kiss her. At first she turns away her head – then, overcome by a fierce impulse of passionate love, she takes his head in both her hands and holds his face close to hers, staring into his eyes. Then she kisses him full on the lips.*]

ANNA [*pushing him away from her – forcing a broken laugh*]: Good-bye.

[*She walks to the doorway in rear – stands with her back toward them, looking out. Her shoulders quiver once or twice as if she were fighting back her sobs.*]

BURKE [*too in the seventh heaven of bliss to get any correct interpretation of her word – with a laugh*]: Good-bye, is it? The divil you say! I'll be coming back at you in a second for more of the same! [*To* CHRIS, *who has quickened to instant attention at his daughter's good-bye, and has looked back at her with a stirring of foolish hope in his eyes.*] Now, me old bucko, what'll you be saying? You heard the words from her own lips. Confess I've bate you. Own up like a man when you're bate fair and square. And here's my hand to you – [*Holds out his hand.*] And let you take it and we'll shake and forget what's over and done, and be friends from this out.

CHRIS [*with implacable hatred*]: Ay don't shake hands with you fallar – not vhile Ay live!

BURKE [*offended*]: The back of my hand to you then, if that suits you better. [*Growling*] 'Tis a rotten bad loser you are, divil mend you!

CHRIS: Ay don't lose – [*Trying to be scornful and self-convincing*] Anna say she like you little bit, but you don't hear her say she marry you, Ay bet. [*At the sound of her name* ANNA *has turned round to them. Her face is composed and calm again, but it is the dead calm of despair.*]

BURKE [*scornfully*]: No, and I wasn't hearing her say the sun is shining either.

CHRIS [*doggedly*]: Dat's all right. She don't say it, yust same.

ANNA [*quietly – coming forward to them*]: No, I didn't say it, Mat.

CHRIS [*eagerly*]: Dere! You hear!

BURKE [*misunderstanding her – with a grin*]: You're waiting till you do be asked, you mane? Well, I'm asking you now. And we'll be married this day, with the help of God!

ANNA [*gently*]: You heard what I said, Mat – after I kissed you?

BURKE [*alarmed by something in her manner*]: No – I disremember.

ANNA: I said good-bye. [*Her voice trembling*] That kiss was for good-bye, Mat.

66

BURKE [*terrified*]: What d'you mane?

ANNA: I can't marry you, Mat – and we've said good-bye. That's all.

CHRIS [*unable to hold back his exultation*]: Ay know it! Ay know dat vas so!

BURKE [*jumping to his feet – unable to believe his ears*]: Anna! Is it making game of me you'd be? 'Tis a quare time to joke with me, and don't be doing it, for the love of God.

ANNA [*looking him in the eyes – steadily*]: D'you think I'd kid you now? No, I'm not joking, Mat. I mean what I said.

BURKE: Ye don't! Ye can't! 'Tis mad you are, I'm telling you!

ANNA [*fixedly*]: No, I'm not.

BURKE [*desperately*]: But what's come over you so sudden? You was saying you loved me –

ANNA: I'll say that as often as you want me to. It's true.

BURKE [*bewildered*]: Then why – what, in the divil's name – Oh, God help me, I can't make head or tail to it at all!

ANNA: Because it's the best way out I can figure, Mat. [*Her voice catching*] I been thinking it over and thinking it over day and night all week. Don't think it ain't hard on me, too, Mat.

BURKE: For the love of God, tell me then, what is it that's preventing you wedding me when the two of us has love? [*Suddenly getting an idea and pointing at* CHRIS – *with exasperation*] Is it giving heed to the like of that old fool ye are, and him hating me and filling your ears full of bloody lies against me?

CHRIS [*getting to his feet – raging triumphantly before* ANNA *has a chance to get in a word*]: Yes, Anna believe me, not you! She know her old fa'der don't lie like you.

ANNA [*turning on her father angrily*]: You sit down, d'you hear? Where do you come in butting in and making things worse? You're like a devil, you are! [*Harshly*] Good Lord, and I was beginning to like you, beginning to forget all I've got held up against you!

CHRIS [crushed – feebly]: You ain't got nutting for hold against me, Anna.

ANNA: Ain't I yust! Well, lemme tell you – [She glances at BURKE and stops abruptly.] Say, Mat, I'm s'prised at you. You didn't think anything he'd said –

BURKE [glumly]: Sure, what else would it be?

ANNA: Think I've ever paid any attention to all his crazy bull? Gee, you must take me for a five-year-old kid.

BURKE [puzzled and beginning to be irritated at her too]: I don't know how to take you, with your saying this one minute and that the next.

ANNA: Well, he has nothing to do with it.

BURKE: Then what is it has? Tell me, and don't keep me waiting and sweating blood.

ANNA [resolutely]: I can't tell you – and I won't. I got a good reason – and that's all you need to know. I can't marry you, that's all there is to it. [Distractedly] So, for Gawd's sake, let's talk of something else.

BURKE: I'll not! [Then fearfully] Is it married to some one else you are – in the West maybe?

ANNA [vehemently]: I should say not.

BURKE [regaining his courage]: To the divil with all other reasons then. They don't matter with me at all. [He gets to his feet confidently, assuming a masterful tone.] I'm thinking you're the like of them women can't make up their mind till they're drove to it. Well, then, I'll make up your mind for you bloody quick. [He takes her by the arms, grinning to soften his serious bullying.] We've had enough of talk! Let you be going into your room now and be dressing in your best and we'll be going ashore.

CHRIS [aroused – angrily]: No, py God, she don't do that! [Takes hold of her arm.]

ANNA [who has listened to BURKE in astonishment. She draws

*away from him, instinctively repelled by his tone, but not exactly
sure if he is serious or not – a trace of resentment in her voice*]:
Say, where do you get that stuff?

BURKE [*imperiously*]: Never mind, now! Let you go get
dressed, I'm saying. [*Then turning to* CHRIS] We'll be seeing
who'll win in the end – me or you.

CHRIS [*to* ANNA – *also in an authoritative tone*]: You stay right
here, Anna, you hear!

[ANNA *stands looking from one to the other of them as if she
thought they had both gone crazy. Then the expression of her
face freezes into the hardened sneer of her experience.*]

BURKE [*violently*]: She'll not! She'll do what I say! You've
had your hold on her long enough. It's my turn now.

ANNA [*with a hard laugh*]: Your turn? Say, what am I, anyway?

BURKE: 'Tis not what you are, 'tis what you're going to be
this day – and that's wedded to me before night comes.
Hurry up now with your dressing.

CHRIS [*commandingly*]: You don't do one tang he say, Anna!
[ANNA *laughs mockingly.*]

BURKE: She will, so!

CHRIS: Ay tal you she don't! Ay'm her fa'der.

BURKE: She will in spite of you. She's taking my orders from
this out, not yours.

ANNA [*laughing again*]: Orders is good!

BURKE [*turning to her impatiently*]: Hurry up now, and shake a
leg. We've no time to be wasting. [*Irritated as she doesn't
move*] Do you hear what I'm telling you?

CHRIS: You stay dere, Anna!

ANNA [*at the end of her patience – blazing out at them passionately*]: You can go to hell, both of you! [*There is something in her tone that makes them forget their quarrel and turn to
her in a stunned amazement.* ANNA *laughs wildly.*] You're just
like all the rest of them – you two! Gawd, you'd think I was
a piece of furniture! I'll show you! Sit down now! [*As they*

hesitate – furiously] Sit down and let me talk for a minute. You're all wrong, see? Listen to me! I'm going to tell you something – and then I'm going to beat it. [*To* BURKE – *with a harsh laugh*] I'm going to tell you a funny story, so pay attention. [*Pointing to* CHRIS] I've been meaning to turn it loose on him every time he'd get my goat with his bull about keeping me safe inland. I wasn't going to tell you, but you've forced me into it. What's the dif? It's all wrong anyway, and you might as well get cured that way as any other. [*With hard mocking*] Only don't forget what you said a minute ago about it not mattering to you what other reason I got so long as I wasn't married to no one else.

BURKE [*manfully*]: That's my word, and I'll stick to it!

ANNA [*laughing bitterly*]: What a chance! You make me laugh, honest! Want to bet you will? Wait 'n' see! [*She stands at the table rear, looking from one to the other of the two men with her hard, mocking smile. Then she begins, fighting to control her emotion and speak calmly.*] First thing is, I want to tell you two guys something. You was going on 's if one of you had got to own me. But nobody owns me, see? – 'cepting myself. I'll do what I please, and no man, I don't give a hoot who he is, can tell me what to do! I ain't asking either of you for a living. I can make it myself – one way or other. I'm my own boss. So put that in your pipe and smoke it! You and your orders!

BURKE [*protestingly*]: I wasn't meaning it that way at all and well you know it. You've no call to be raising this rumpus with me. [*Pointing to* CHRIS] 'Tis him you've a right –

ANNA: I'm coming to him. But you – you did mean it that way, too. You sounded – yust like all the rest. [*Hysterically*] But, damn it, shut up! Let me talk for a change!

BURKE: 'Tis quare, rough talk, that – for a dacent girl the like of you!

ANNA [*with a hard laugh*]: Decent? Who told you I was?

[CHRIS *is sitting with bowed shoulders, his head in his hands. She leans over in exasperation and shakes him violently by the shoulder.*] Don't go to sleep, Old Man! Listen here, I'm talking to you now!

CHRIS [*straightening up and looking about as if he were seeking a way to escape – with frightened foreboding in his voice*]: Ay don't vant for hear it. You vas going out of head, Ay tank, Anna.

ANNA [*violently*]: Well, living with you is enough to drive anyone off their nut. Your bunk about the farm being so fine! Didn't I write you year after year how rotten it was and what a dirty slave them cousins made of me? What'd you care? Nothing! Not even enough to come out and see me! That crazy bull about wanting to keep me away from the sea don't go down with me! You yust didn't want to be bothered with me! You're like all the rest of 'em!

CHRIS [*feebly*]: Anna! It ain't so –

ANNA [*not heeding his interruption – revengefully*]: But one thing I never wrote you. It was one of them cousins that you think is such nice people – the youngest son – Paul – that started me wrong. [*Loudly*] It wasn't none of my fault. I hated him worse'n hell, and he knew it. But he was big and strong – [*pointing to* BURKE] – like you!

BURKE [*half-springing to his feet – his fists clenched*]: God blarst it! [*He sinks slowly back in his chair again, the knuckles showing white on his clenched hands, his face tense with the effort to suppress his grief and rage.*]

CHRIS [*in a cry of horrified pain*]: Anna!

ANNA [*to him – seeming not to have heard their interruptions*]: That was why I run away from the farm. That was what made me get a yob as nurse girl in St Paul. [*With a hard, mocking laugh*] And you think that was a nice yob for a girl, too, don't you? [*Sarcastically*] With all them nice inland fellers yust looking for a chance to marry me, I s'pose. Marry me? What a chance! They wasn't looking for marrying. [*As*

BURKE *lets a groan of fury escape him – desperately*] I'm own-ing up to everything fair and square. I was caged in, I tell you – yust like in yail – taking care of other people's kids – listening to 'em bawling and crying day and night – when I wanted to be out – and I was lonesome as hell! [*With a sudden weariness in her voice*] So I give up finally. What was the use? [*She stops and looks at the two men. Both are motion-less and silent.* CHRIS *seems in a stupor of despair, his house of cards fallen about him.* BURKE'S *face is livid with the rage that is eating him up, but he is too stunned and bewildered yet to find a vent for it. The condemnation she feels in their silence goads* ANNA *into a harsh, strident defiance.*] You don't say nothing – either of you – but I know what you're thinking. You're like all the rest! [*To* CHRIS *– furiously*] And who's to blame for it, me or you? If you'd ever acted like a man – if you'd ever been a regular father and had me with you – maybe things would be different!

CHRIS [*in agony*]: Don't talk dat vay, Anna! Ay go crazy! Ay von't listen! [*Puts his hands over his ears.*]

ANNA [*infuriated by his action – stridently*]: You will listen though! [*She leans over and pulls his hands from his ears – with hysterical rage.*] You – keeping me safe inland – I wasn't no nurse girl the last two years – I lied when I wrote you – I was in a house, that's what! – yes, that kind of a house – the kind sailors like you and Mat goes to in port – and your nice inland men, too – and all men, God damn 'em! I hate 'em! Hate 'em! [*She breaks into hysterical sobbing, throwing herself into the chair and hiding her face in her hands on the table. The two men have sprung to their feet.*]

CHRIS [*whimpering like a child*]: Anna! Anna! It's lie! It's lie! [*He stands wringing his hands together and begins to weep.*]

BURKE [*his whole great body tense like a spring – dully and gropingly*]: So that's what's in it!

ANNA [*raising her head at the sound of his voice – with extreme mocking bitterness*]: I s'pose you remember your promise,

Mat? No other reason was to count with you so long as I wasn't married already. So I s'pose you want me to get dressed and go ashore, don't you? [*She laughs.*] Yes, you do!

BURKE [*on the verge of his outbreak – stammering*]: God stiffen you!

ANNA [*trying to keep up her hard, bitter tone, but gradually letting a note of pitiful pleading creep in*]: I s'pose if I tried to tell you I wasn't – that – no more you'd believe me, wouldn't you? Yes, you would! And if I told you that yust getting out in this barge, and being on the sea had changed me and made me feel different about things, 's if all I'd been through wasn't me and didn't count and was yust like it never happened – you'd laugh, wouldn't you? And you'd die laughing sure if I said that meeting you that funny way that night in the fog, and afterwards seeing that you was straight goods stuck on me, had got me to thinking for the first time, and I sized you up as a different kind of man – a sea-man as different from the ones on land as water is from mud – and that was why I got stuck on you, too. I wanted to marry you and fool you, but I couldn't. Don't you see how I'd changed? I couldn't marry you with you believing a lie – and I was shamed to tell you the truth – till the both of you forced my hand, and I seen you was the same as all the rest. And now, give me a bawling out and beat it, like I can tell you're going to. [*She stops, looking at* BURKE. *He is silent, his face averted, his features beginning to work with fury. She pleads passionately.*] Will you believe it if I tell you that loving you has made me – clean? It's the straight goods, honest! [*Then as he doesn't reply – bitterly*] Like hell you will! You're like all the rest!

BURKE [*blazing out – turning on her in a perfect frenzy of rage – his voice trembling with passion*]: The rest, is it? God's curse on you! Clane, is it? You slut, you, I'll be killing you now! [*He picks up the chair on which he has been sitting, and, swinging it high over his shoulder, springs toward her.* CHRIS *rushes forward with a cry of alarm, trying to ward off the blow from his daughter.* ANNA *looks up into* BURKE'S *eyes with the fearlessness of despair.* BURKE *checks himself, the chair held in the air.*]

CHRIS [*wildly*]: Stop, you crazy fool! You vant for murder her?

ANNA [*pushing her father away brusquely, her eyes still holding* BURKE'S]: Keep out of this, you! [*To* BURKE – *dully*] Well, ain't you got the nerve to do it? Go ahead! I'll be thankful to you, honest. I'm sick of the whole game.

BURKE [*throwing the chair away into a corner of the room – helplessly*]: I can't do it, God help me, and your two eyes looking at me. [*Furiously*] Though I do be thinking I'd have a good right to smash your skull like a rotten egg. Was there iver a woman in the world had the rottenness in her that you have, and was there iver a man the like of me was made the fool of the world, and me thinking thoughts about you, and having great love for you, and dreaming dreams of the fine life we'd have when we'd be wedded! [*His voice high-pitched in a lamentation that is like a keen*] Yerra, God help me! I'm destroyed entirely and my heart is broken in bits! I'm asking God Himself, was it for this He'd have me roaming the earth since I was a lad only, to come to black shame in the end, where I'd be giving a power of love to a woman is the same as others you'd meet in any hooker-shanty in port, with red gowns on them and paint on their grinning mugs, would be sleeping with any man for a dollar or two!

ANNA [*in a scream*]: Don't, Mat! For Gawd's sake! [*Then raging and pounding on the table with her hands*] Get out of here! Leave me alone! Get out of here!

BURKE [*his anger rushing back on him*]: I'll be going, surely! And I'll be drinking sloos of whisky will wash that black kiss of yours off my lips; and I'll be getting dead rotten drunk so I'll not remember if 'twas iver born you was at all; and

I'll be shipping away on some boat will take me to the other end of the world where I'll never see your face again! [*He turns toward the door.*]

CHRIS [*who has been standing in a stupor – suddenly grasping* BURKE *by the arm – stupidly*]: No, you don't go. Ay tank maybe it's better Anna marry you now.

BURKE [*shaking* CHRIS *off – furiously*]: Lave go of me, ye old ape! Marry her, is it? I'd see her roasting in hell first! I'm shipping away out of this, I'm telling you! [*Pointing to* ANNA *– passionately*] And my curse on you and the curse of Almighty God and all the Saints! You've destroyed me this day, and may you lie awake in the long nights, tormented with thoughts of Mat Burke and the great wrong you've done him!

ANNA [*in anguish*]: Mat! [*But he turns without another word and strides out of the doorway.* ANNA *looks after him wildly, starts to run after him, then hides her face in her outstretched arms, sobbing.* CHRIS *stands in a stupor, staring at the floor.*]

CHRIS [*after a pause, dully*]: Ay tank Ay go ashore, too.

ANNA [*looking up, wildly*]: Not after him! Let him go! Don't you dare –

CHRIS [*sombrely*]: Ay go for gat drink.

ANNA [*with a harsh laugh*]: So I'm driving you to drink, too, eh? I s'pose you want to get drunk so's you can forget – like him?

CHRIS [*bursting out angrily*]: Yes, Ay vant! You tank Ay like hear dem tangs. [*Breaking down – weeping*] Ay tank you vasn't dat kind of gel, Anna.

ANNA [*mockingly*]: And I s'pose you want me to beat it, don't you? You don't want me here disgracing you, I s'pose?

CHRIS: No, you stay here! [*Goes over and pats her on the shoulder, the tears running down his face.*] Ain't your fault, Anna, Ay know dat. [*She looks up at him, softened. He bursts into rage.*] It's dat ole davil, sea, do this to me! [*He shakes his fist at the door.*] It's her dirty tricks! It vas all right on barge with yust you and me. Den she bring dat Irish fallar in fog, she make you like him, she make you fight with me all time! If dat Irish fallar don't never come, you don't never tal me dem tangs, Ay don't never know, and everytang's all right. [*He shakes his fist again.*] Dirty ole davil!

ANNA [*with spent weariness*]: Oh, what's the use? Go on ashore and get drunk.

CHRIS [*goes into room on left and gets his cap. He goes to the door, silent and stupid – then turns*]: You vait here, Anna?

ANNA [*dully*]: Maybe – and maybe not. Maybe I'll get drunk, too. Maybe I'll – But what the hell do you care what I do? Go on and beat it. [CHRIS *turns stupidly and goes out.* ANNA *sits at the table, staring straight in front of her.*]

THE CURTAIN FALLS

ACT FOUR

Same as Act Three, about nine o'clock of a foggy night two days later. The whistles of steamers in the harbour can be heard. The cabin is lighted by a small lamp on the table. A suitcase stands in the middle of the floor.

> [ANNA *is sitting in the rocking-chair. She wears a hat, is all dressed up as in Act One. Her face is pale, looks terribly tired and worn, as if the two days just past had been ones of suffering and sleepless nights. She stares before her despondently, her chin in her hands. There is a timid knock on the door in rear.* ANNA *jumps to her feet with a startled exclamation and looks toward the door with an expression of mingled hope and fear.*]

ANNA [*faintly*]: Come in. [*Then summoning her courage – more resolutely*] Come in. [*The door is opened and* CHRIS *appears in the doorway. He is in a very bleary, bedraggled condition, suffering from the after-effects of his drink. A tin pail full of foaming beer is in his hand. He comes forward, his eyes avoiding* ANNA'S. *He mutters stupidly,* 'It's foggy.']

ANNA [*looking him over with contempt*]: So you come back at last, did you? You're a fine-looking sight! [*Then jeeringly*] I thought you'd beaten it for good on account of the disgrace I'd brought on you.

CHRIS [*wincing – faintly*]: Don't say dat, Anna, please! [*He sits in a chair by the table, setting down the can of beer, holding his head in his hands.*]

ANNA [*looks at him with a certain sympathy*]: What's the trouble? Feeling sick?

CHRIS [*dully*]: Inside my head feel sick.

ANNA: Well, what d'you expect after being soused for two days? [*Resentfully*] It serves you right. A fine thing – you leaving me alone on this barge all that time!

77

CHRIS [*humbly*]: Ay'm sorry, Anna.

ANNA [*scornfully*]: Sorry!

CHRIS: But Ay'm not sick inside head vay you mean. Ay'm sick from tank too much about you, about me.

ANNA: And how about me? D'you suppose I ain't been thinking, too?

CHRIS: Ay'm sorry, Anna. [*He sees her bag and gives a start.*] You pack your bag, Anna? You vas going –

ANNA [*forcibly*]: Yes, I was going right back to what you think.

CHRIS: Anna!

ANNA: I went ashore to get a train for New York. I'd been waiting and waiting till I was sick of it. Then I changed my mind and decided not to go today. But I'm going first thing tomorrow, so it'll all be the same in the end.

CHRIS [*raising his head – pleadingly*]: No, you never do dat, Anna!

ANNA [*with a sneer*]: Why not, I'd like to know?

CHRIS: You don't never gat to do – dat way – no more, Ay tal you. Ay fix dat up all right.

ANNA [*suspiciously*]: Fix what up?

CHRIS [*not seeming to have heard her question – sadly*]: You vas vaiting, you say? You vasn't vaiting for me, Ay bet.

ANNA [*callously*]: You'd win.

CHRIS: For dat Irish fallar?

ANNA [*defiantly*]: Yes – if you want to know! [*Then with a forlorn laugh*] If he did come back it'd only be 'cause he wanted to beat me up or kill me, I suppose. But even if he did, I'd rather have him come than not show up at all. I wouldn't care what he did.

CHRIS: Ay guess it's true you vas in love with him all right.

ANNA: You guess!

CHRIS [*turning to her earnestly*]: And Ay'm sorry for you like hell he don't come, Anna!

ANNA [*softened*]: Seems to me you've changed your tune a lot.

78

CHRIS: Ay've been tanking, and Ay guess it vas all my fault –
all bad tangs dat happen to you. [*Pleadingly*] You try for not
hate me, Anna. Ay'm crazy ole fool, dat's all.

ANNA: Who said I hated you?

CHRIS: Ay'm sorry for everytang Ay do wrong for you,
Anna. Ay vant for you be happy all rest of your life for
make up! It make you happy marry dat Irish fallar, Ay vant
it, too.

ANNA [*dully*]: Well, there ain't no chance. But I'm glad you
think different about it, anyway.

CHRIS [*supplicatingly*]: And you tank – maybe – you forgive
me sometime?

ANNA [*with a wan smile*]: I'll forgive you right now.

CHRIS [*seizing her hand and kissing it – brokenly*]: Anna lilla!
Anna lilla!

ANNA [*touched but a bit embarrassed*]: Don't bawl about it.
There ain't nothing to forgive, anyway. It ain't your fault,
and it ain't mine, and it ain't his neither. We're all poor
nuts, and things happen, and we yust get mixed in wrong,
that's all.

CHRIS [*eagerly*]: You say right tang, Anna, py golly! It ain't
nobody's fault! [*Shaking his fist*] It's dat ole davil, sea!

ANNA [*with an exasperated laugh*]: Gee, won't you ever can
that stuff? [CHRIS *relapses into injured silence. After a pause*
ANNA *continues curiously.*] You said a minute ago you'd
fixed something up – about me. What was it?

CHRIS [*after a hesitating pause*]: Ay'm shipping avay on sea
again, Anna.

ANNA [*astounded*]: You're – what?

CHRIS: Ay sign on steamer sail tomorrow. Ay gat my ole
yob – bos'n. [ANNA *stares at him. As he goes on, a bitter smile
comes over her face.*] Ay tank dat's best tang for you. Ay
only bring you bad luck, Ay tank. Ay make your mo'der's
life sorry. Ay don't vant make yours dat way, but Ay do
yust same. Dat ole davil, sea, she make me Yonah man ain't

79

no good for nobody. And Ay tank now it ain't no use fight with sea. No man dat live going to beat her, py yingo!

ANNA [*with a laugh of helpless bitterness*]: So that's how you've fixed me, is it?

CHRIS: Yes, Ay tank if dat ole davil gat me back she leave you alone den.

ANNA [*bitterly*]: But, for Gawd's sake, don't you see, you're doing the same thing you've always done? Don't you see – [*But she sees the look of obsessed stubbornness on her father's face and gives it up helplessly.*] But what's the use of talking. You ain't right, that's what. I'll never blame you for nothing no more. But how you could figure out that was fixing me –

CHRIS: Dat ain't all. Ay gat dem fallars in steamship office to pay you all money coming to me every month vhile Ay'm avay.

ANNA [*with a hard laugh*]: Thanks. But I guess I won't be hard up for no small change.

CHRIS [*hurt – humbly*]: It ain't much, Ay know, but it's plenty for keep you so you never gat go back –

ANNA [*shortly*]: Shut up, will you! We'll talk about it later, see?

CHRIS [*after a pause – ingratiatingly*]: You like Ay go ashore look for dat Irish fallar, Anna?

ANNA [*angrily*]: Not much! Think I want to drag him back?

CHRIS [*after a pause – uncomfortably*]: Py golly, dat booze don't go vell. Give me fever, Ay tank. Ay feel hot like hell. [*He takes off his coat and lets it drop on the floor. There is a loud thud.*]

ANNA [*with a start*]: What you got in your pocket, for Pete's sake – a ton of lead? [*She reaches down, takes the coat and pulls out a revolver – looks from it to him in amazement.*] A gun? What were you doing with this?

CHRIS [*sheepishly*]: Ay forgat. Ain't nutting. Ain't loaded, anyway.

ANNA [*breaking it open to make sure – then closing it again – look-*

ing at him suspiciously]: That ain't telling me why you got it?

CHRIS [*sheepishly*]: Ay'm ole fool. Ay gat it vhen Ay go ashore first. Ay tank den it's all fault of dat Irish fallar.

ANNA [*with a shudder*]: Say, you're crazier than I thought. I never dreamt you'd go that far.

CHRIS [*quickly*]: Ay don't. Ay gat better sense right avay. Ay don't never buy bullets even. It ain't his fault, Ay know.

ANNA [*still suspicious of him*]: Well, I'll take care of this for a while, loaded or not. [*She puts it in the drawer of table and closes the drawer.*]

CHRIS [*placatingly*]: Throw it overboard if you vant. Ay don't care. [*Then after a pause*] Py golly, Ay tank Ay go lie down. Ay feel sick. [ANNA *takes a magazine from the table.* CHRIS *hesitates by her chair.*] Ve talk again before Ay go, yes?

ANNA [*dully*]: Where's this ship going to?

CHRIS: Cape Town. Dat's in South Africa. She's British steamer called *Londonderry*. [*He stands hesitatingly – finally blurts out*] Anna – you forgive me sure?

ANNA [*wearily*]: Sure I do. You ain't to blame. You're yust – what you are – like me.

CHRIS [*pleadingly*]: Den – you lat me kiss you again once?

ANNA [*raising her face – forcing a wan smile*]: Sure. No hard feelings.

CHRIS [*kisses her – brokenly*]: Anna lilla! Ay – [*he fights for words to express himself, but finds none – miserably – with a sob*] – Ay can't say it. Good night, Anna.

ANNA: Good night. [*He picks up the can of beer and goes slowly into the room on left, his shoulders bowed, his head sunk forward dejectedly. He closes the door after him.* ANNA *turns over the pages of the magazine, trying desperately to banish her thoughts by looking at the pictures. This fails to distract her, and flinging the magazine back on the table, she springs to her feet and walks about the cabin distractedly, clenching and unclenching her hands. She speaks aloud to herself in a tense, trembling voice.*] Gawd, I can't stand this much longer! What am I waiting for, anyway? – like a damn fool! [*She laughs helplessly, then checks herself abruptly, as she hears the sound of heavy footsteps on the deck outside. She appears to recognize these and her face lights up with joy. She gasps:*] Mat!

[*A strange terror seems suddenly to seize her. She rushes to the table, takes the revolver out of drawer, and crouches down in the corner, left, behind the cupboard. A moment later the door is flung open and* MAT BURKE *appears in the doorway. He is in bad shape – his clothes torn and dirty, covered with sawdust as if he had been grovelling or sleeping on bar-room floors. There is a red bruise on his forehead over one of his eyes, another over one cheekbone, his knuckles are skinned and raw – plain evidence of the fighting he has been through on his 'bat'. His eyes are bloodshot and heavy-lidded, his face has a bloated look. But beyond these appearances – the results of heavy drinking – there is an expression in his eyes of wild mental turmoil, of impotent animal rage baffled by its own abject misery.*]

BURKE [*peers blinkingly about the cabin – hoarsely*]: Let you not be hiding from me, whoever's here – though 'tis well you know I'd have a right to come back and murder you. [*He stops to listen. Hearing no sound, he closes the door behind him and comes forward to the table. He throws himself into the rocking-chair – despondently*] There's no one here, I'm thinking, and 'tis a great fool I am to be coming. [*With a sort of dumb, uncomprehending anguish*] Yerra, Mat Burke, 'tis a great jackass you've become and what's got into you at all, at all? She's gone out of this long ago, I'm telling you, and you'll never see her face again. [ANNA *stands up, hesitating, struggling between joy and fear.* BURKE'S *eyes fall on* ANNA'S *bag. He leans over to examine it.*] What's this? [*Joyfully*] It's hers. She's not gone! But where is she? Ashore? [*Darkly*] What would she be doing ashore on this rotten night?

[*His face suddenly convulsed with grief and rage*] 'Tis that, is it? Oh, God's curse on her! [*Raging*] I'll wait till she comes and choke her dirty life out.

    [ANNA *starts, her face grows hard. She steps into the room, the revolver in her right hand by her side.*]

ANNA [*in a cold, hard tone*]: What are you doing here?

BURKE [*wheeling about with a terrified gasp*]: Glory be to God! [*They remain motionless and silent for a moment, holding each other's eyes.*]

ANNA [*in the same hard voice*]: Well, can't you talk?

BURKE [*trying to fall into an easy, careless tone*]: You've a year's growth scared out of me, coming at me so sudden and me thinking I was alone.

ANNA: You've got your nerve butting in here without knocking or nothing. What d'you want?

BURKE [*airily*]: Oh, nothing much. I was wanting to have a last word with you, that's all. [*He moves a step toward her.*]

ANNA [*sharply – raising the revolver in her hand*]: Careful now! Don't try getting too close. I heard what you said you'd do to me.

BURKE [*noticing the revolver for the first time*]: Is it murdering me you'd be now, God forgive you? [*Then with a contemptuous laugh*] Or is it thinking I'd be frightened by that old tin whistle? [*He walks straight for her.*]

ANNA [*wildly*]: Look out, I tell you!

BURKE [*who has come so close that the revolver is almost touching his chest*]: Let you shoot, then! [*Then with sudden wild grief*] Let you shoot, I'm saying, and be done with it! Let you end me with a shot and I'll be thanking you, for it's a rotten dog's life I've lived the past two days since I've known what you are, till I'm after wishing I was never born at all!

ANNA [*overcome – letting the revolver drop to the floor, as if her fingers had no strength to hold it – hysterically*]: What d'you want coming here? Why don't you beat it? Go on! [*She passes him and sinks down in the rocking-chair.*]

BURKE [*following her – mournfully*]: 'Tis right you'd be asking why did I come. [*Then angrily*] 'Tis because 'tis a great weak fool of the world I am, and me tormented with the wickedness you'd told of yourself, and drinking oceans of booze that'd make me forget. Forget? Divil a word I'd forget, and your face grinning always in front of my eyes, awake or asleep, till I do be thinking a madhouse is the proper place for me.

ANNA [*glancing at his hands and face – scornfully*]: You look like you ought to be put away some place. Wonder you wasn't pulled in. You been scrapping, too, ain't you?

BURKE: I have – with every scut would take off his coat to me! [*Fiercely*] And each time I'd be hitting one a clout in the mug, it wasn't his face I'd be seeing at all, but yours, and me wanting to drive you a blow would knock you out of this world where I wouldn't be seeing or thinking more of you.

ANNA [*her lips trembling pitifully*]: Thanks!

BURKE [*walking up and down – distractedly*]: That's right, make game of me! Oh, I'm a great coward surely, to be coming back to speak with you at all. You've a right to laugh at me.

ANNA: I ain't laughing at you, Mat.

BURKE [*unheeding*]: You to be what you are, and me to be Mat Burke, and me to be drove back to look at you again! 'Tis black shame is on me!

ANNA [*resentfully*]: Then get out. No one's holding you!

BURKE [*bewilderedly*]: And me to listen to that talk from a woman like you and be frightened to close her mouth with a slap! Oh, God help me, I'm a yellow coward for all men to spit at! [*Then furiously*] But I'll not be getting out of this till I've had me word. [*Raising his fist threateningly*] And let you look out how you'd drive me! [*Letting his fist fall helplessly*] Don't be angry now! I'm raving like a real lunatic, I'm thinking, and the sorrow you put on me has my brains drownded in grief. [*Suddenly bending down to her and grasping her arm intensely*] Tell me it's a lie, I'm saying! That's what I'm after coming to hear you say.

ANNA [*dully*]: A lie? What?

BURKE [*with passionate entreaty*]: All the badness you told me two days back. Sure it must be a lie! You was only making game of me, wasn't you? Tell me 'twas a lie, Anna, and I'll be saying prayers of thanks on my two knees to the Almighty God!

ANNA [*terribly shaken – faintly*]: I can't, Mat. [*As he turns away – imploringly*] Oh, Mat, won't you see that no matter what I was I ain't that any more? Why, listen! I packed up my bag this afternoon and went ashore. I'd been waiting here all alone for two days, thinking maybe you'd come back – thinking maybe you'd think over all I'd said – and maybe – oh, I don't know what I was hoping! But I was afraid to even go out of the cabin for a second, honest – afraid you might come and not find me here. Then I gave up hope when you didn't show up and I went to the railroad station. I was going to New York. I was going back –

BURKE [*hoarsely*]: God's curse on you!

ANNA: Listen, Mat! You hadn't come, and I'd gave up hope. But – in the station – I couldn't go. I'd bought my ticket and everything. [*She takes the ticket from her dress and tries to hold it before his eyes.*] But I got to thinking about you – and I couldn't take the train – I couldn't! So I come back here – to wait some more. Oh, Mat, don't you see I've changed? Can't you forgive what's dead and gone – and forget it?

BURKE [*turning on her – overcome by rage again*]: Forget, is it? I'll not forget till my dying day, I'm telling you, and me tormented with thoughts. [*In a frenzy*] Oh, I'm wishing I had wan of them fornest me this minute and I'd beat him with my fists till he'd be a bloody corpse! I'm wishing the whole lot of them will roast in hell till the Judgement Day – and yourself along with them, for you're as bad as they are.

ANNA [*shuddering*]: Mat! [*Then after a pause – in a voice of dead, stony calm*] Well, you've had your say. Now you better beat it.

BURKE [*starts slowly for the door – hesitates – then after a pause*]: And what'll you be doing?

ANNA: What difference does it make to you?

BURKE: I'm asking you!

ANNA [*in the same tone*]: My bag's packed and I got my ticket. I'll go to New York tomorrow.

BURKE [*helplessly*]: You mean – you'll be doing the same again?

ANNA [*stonily*]: Yes.

BURKE [*in anguish*]: You'll not! Don't torment me with that talk! 'Tis a she-devil you are sent to drive me mad entirely!

ANNA [*her voice breaking*]: Oh, for Gawd's sake, Mat, leave me alone! Go away! Don't you see I'm licked? Why d'you want to keep on kicking me?

BURKE [*indignantly*]: And don't you deserve the worst I'd say, God forgive you?

ANNA: All right. Maybe I do. But don't rub it in. Why ain't you done what you said you was going to? Why ain't you got that ship was going to take you to the other side of the earth where you'd never see me again?

BURKE: I have.

ANNA [*startled*]: What – then you're going – honest?

BURKE: I signed on today at noon, drunk as I was – and she's sailing tomorrow.

ANNA: And where's she going to?

BURKE: Cape Town.

ANNA [*the memory of having heard that name a little while before coming to her – with a start, confusedly*]: Cape Town? Where's that? Far away?

BURKE: 'Tis at the end of Africa. That's far for you.

ANNA [*forcing a laugh*]: You're keeping your word all right, ain't you? [*After a slight pause – curiously*] What's the boat's name?

BURKE: The *Londonderry*.

ANNA [*it suddenly comes to her that this is the same ship her father is sailing on*]: The *Londonderry*! It's the same – oh, this is too much! [*With wild, ironical laughter*] Ha-ha-ha!

BURKE: What's up with you now!

ANNA: Ha-ha-ha! It's funny, funny! I'll die laughing!

BURKE [*irritated*]: Laughing at what?

ANNA: It's a secret. You'll know soon enough. It's funny. [*Controlling herself – after a pause – cynically*] What kind of a place is this Cape Town? Plenty of dames there, I suppose?

BURKE: To hell with them! That I may never see another woman to my dying hour!

ANNA: That's what you say now, but I'll bet by the time you get there you'll have forgot all about me and start in talking the same old bull you talked to me to the first one you meet.

BURKE [*offended*]: I'll not, then! God mend you, is it making me out to be the like of yourself you are, and you taking up with this one and that all the years of your life?

ANNA [*angrily assertive*]: Yes, that's yust what I do mean! You been doing the same thing all your life, picking up a new girl in every port. How're you any better than I was?

BURKE [*thoroughly exasperated*]: Is it no shame you have at all? I'm a fool to be wasting talk on you and you hardened in badness. I'll go out of this and lave you alone for ever. [*He starts for the door – then stops to turn on her furiously.*] And I suppose 'tis the same lies you told them all before that you told to me?

ANNA [*indignantly*]: That's a lie! I never did!

BURKE [*miserably*]: You'd be saying that, anyway.

ANNA [*forcibly, with growing intensity*]: Are you trying to accuse me – of being in love – really in love – with them?

BURKE: I'm thinking you were, surely.

ANNA [*furiously, as if this were the last insult – advancing on him threateningly*]: You mutt, you! I've stood enough from you. Don't you dare. [*With scornful bitterness*] Love 'em! Oh, my Gawd! You damn thick-head! Love 'em? [*Savagely*] I hated 'em, I tell you! Hated 'em, hated 'em, hated 'em! And may Gawd strike me dead this minute and my mother, too, if she was alive, if I ain't telling you the honest truth!

BURKE [*immensely pleased by her vehemence – a light beginning to break over his face – but still uncertain, torn between doubt and the desire to believe – helplessly*]: If I could only be believing you now!

ANNA [*distractedly*]: Oh, what's the use? What's the use of me talking? What's the use of anything? [*Pleadingly*] Oh, Mat, you mustn't think that for a second! You mustn't! Think all the other bad about me you want to, and I won't kick, 'cause you've a right to. But don't think that! [*On the point of tears*] I couldn't bear it! It'd be yust too much to know you was going away where I'd never see you again – thinking that about me!

BURKE [*after an inward struggle – tensely – forcing out the words with difficulty*]: If I was believing – that you'd never had love for any other man in the world but me – I could be forgetting the rest, maybe.

ANNA [*with a cry of joy*]: Mat!

BURKE [*slowly*]: If 'tis truth you're after telling, I'd have a right, maybe, to believe you'd changed – and that I'd changed you myself till the thing you'd been all your life wouldn't be you any more at all.

ANNA [*hanging on his words – breathlessly*]: Oh, Mat! That's what I been trying to tell you all along!

BURKE [*simply*]: For I've a power of strength in me to lead men the way I want, and women, too, maybe, and I'm thinking I'd change you to a new woman entirely, so I'd never know, or you either, what kind of woman you'd been in the past at all.

ANNA: Yes, you could, Mat! I know you could!

BURKE: And I'm thinking 'twasn't your fault, maybe, but having that old ape for a father that left you to grow up alone, made you what you was. And if I could be believing 'tis only me you –

ANNA [*distractedly*]: You got to believe it, Mat! What can I do? I'll do anything, anything you want to prove I'm not lying!

BURKE [*suddenly seems to have a solution. He feels in the pocket of his coat and grasps something – solemnly*]: Would you be willing to swear an oath, now – a terrible, fearful oath would send your soul to the divils in hell if you was lying?

ANNA [*eagerly*]: Sure, I'll swear, Mat – on anything!

BURKE [*takes a small, cheap old crucifix from his pocket and holds it up for her to see*]: Will you swear on this?

ANNA [*reaching out for it*]: Yes. Sure I will. Give it to me.

BURKE [*holding it away*]: 'Tis a cross was given me by my mother, God rest her soul. [*He makes the sign of the cross mechanically.*] I was a lad only, and she told me to keep it by me if I'd be waking or sleeping and never lose it, and it'd being me luck. She died soon after. But I'm after keeping it with me from that day to this, and I'm telling you there's great power in it, and 'tis great bad luck it's saved me from and me roaming the seas, and I having it tied round my neck when my last ship sunk, and it bringing me safe to land when the others went to their death. [*Very earnestly*] And I'm warning you now, if you'd swear an oath on this, 'tis my old woman herself will be looking down from Hivin above, and praying Almighty God and the Saints to put a great curse on you if she'd hear you swearing a lie!

ANNA [*awed by his manner – superstitiously*]: I wouldn't have the nerve – honest – if it was a lie. But it's the truth and I ain't scared to swear. Give it to me.

BURKE [*handing it to her – almost frightened, as if he feared for her safety*]: Be careful what you'd swear, I'm saying.

ANNA [*holding the cross gingerly*]: Well – what do you want me to swear? You say it.

BURKE: Swear I'm the only man in the world ivir you felt love for.

ANNA [*looking into his eyes steadily*]: I swear it.

BURKE: And that you'll be forgetting from this day all the badness you've done and never do the like of it again.

ANNA [*forcibly*]: I swear it! I swear it by God!

BURKE: And may the blackest curse of God strike you if you're lying. Say it now!

ANNA: And may the blackest curse of God strike me if I'm lying!

BURKE [*with a stupendous sigh*]: Oh, glory be to God, I'm after believing you now! [*He takes the cross from her hand, his face beaming with joy, and puts it back in his pocket. He puts his arm about her waist and is about to kiss her when he stops, appalled by some terrible doubt.*]

ANNA [*alarmed*]: What's the matter with you?

BURKE [*with sudden fierce questioning*]: Is it Catholic ye are?

ANNA [*confused*]: No. Why?

BURKE [*filled with a sort of bewildered foreboding*]: Oh, God, help me! [*With a dark glance of suspicion at her*] There's some divil's trickery in it, to be swearing an oath on a Catholic cross and you wan of the others.

ANNA [*distractedly*]: Oh, Mat, don't you believe me?

BURKE [*miserably*]: If it isn't a Catholic you are –

ANNA: I ain't nothing. What's the difference? Didn't you hear me swear?

BURKE [*passionately*]: Oh, I'd a right to stay away from you – but I couldn't! I was loving you in spite of it all, and wanting to be with you, God forgive me, no matter what you are. I'd go mad if I'd not have you! I'd be killing the world – [*He seizes her in his arms and kisses her fiercely.*]

ANNA [*with a gasp of joy*]: Mat!

BURKE [*suddenly holding her away from him and staring into her eyes as if to probe into her soul – slowly*]: If your oath is no proper oath at all, I'll have to be taking your naked word for it and have you anyway, I'm thinking – I'm needing you that bad!

ANNA [*hurt – reproachfully*]: Mat! I swore, didn't I?

BURKE [*defiantly, as if challenging fate*]: Oath or no oath, 'tis no matter. We'll be wedded in the morning, with the help of God. [*Still more defiantly*] We'll be happy now, the two of us, in spite of the divil!

[*He crushes her to him and kisses her again. The door on the left is pushed open and* CHRIS *appears in the doorway. He stands blinking at them. At first the old expression of hatred of* BURKE *comes into his eyes instinctively. Then a look of resignation and relief takes its place. His face lights up with a sudden happy thought. He turns back into the bedroom – reappears immediately with the tin can of beer in his hand – grinning.*]

CHRIS: Ve have drink on this, py golly! [*They break away from each other with startled exclamations.*]

BURKE [*explosively*]: God stiffen it! [*He takes a step toward* CHRIS *threateningly.*]

ANNA [*happily – to her father*]: That's the way to talk! [*With a laugh*] And say, it's about time for you and Mat to kiss and make up. You're going to be shipmates on the *Londonderry*, did you know it?

BURKE [*astounded*]: Shipmates – Has himself –

CHRIS [*equally astounded*]: Ay vas bos'n on her.

BURKE: The divil! [*Then angrily*] You'd be going back to sea and leaving her alone, would you?

ANNA [*quickly*]: It's all right, Mat. That's where he belongs, and I want him to go. You got to go, too; we'll need the money. [*With a laugh, as she gets the glasses*] And as for me being alone, that runs in the family, and I'll get used to it. [*Pouring out their glasses*] I'll get a little house some-where, and I'll make a regular place for you two to come back to – wait and see. And now you drink up and be friends.

BURKE [*happily – but still a bit resentful against the old man*]: Sure! [*Clinking his glass against* CHRIS'S] Here's luck to you! [*He drinks.*]

CHRIS [*subdued – his face melancholy*]: Skoal. [*He drinks.*]

BURKE [*to* ANNA, *with a wink*]: You'll not be lonesome long. I'll see to that, with the help of God. 'Tis himself here will be having a grandchild to ride on his foot, I'm telling you!

ANNA [*turning away in embarrassment*]: Quit the kidding, now. [*She picks up her bag and goes into the room on left. As soon as she is gone* BURKE *relapses into an attitude of gloomy thought.* CHRIS *stares at his beer absentmindedly. Finally* BURKE *turns on him.*]

BURKE: Is it any religion at all you have, you and your Anna?

CHRIS [*surprised*]: Vhy yes. Ve vas Lutheran in ole country.

BURKE [*horrified*]: Luthers, is it? [*Then with a grim resignation, slowly, aloud to himself*] Well, I'm damned then surely. Yerra, what's the difference? 'Tis the will of God, anyway.

CHRIS [*moodily preoccupied with his own thoughts – speaks with sombre premonition as* ANNA *re-enters from the left*]: It's funny. It's queer, yes – you and me shipping on same boat dat vay. It ain't right. Ay don't know – it's dat funny vay ole davil sea do her vorst dirty tricks, yes. It's so. [*He gets up and goes back, and opening the door, stares out into the darkness.*]

BURKE [*nodding his head in gloomy acquiescence – with a great sigh*]: I'm fearing maybe you have the right of it for once, divil take you.

ANNA [*forcing a laugh*]: Gee, Mat, you ain't agreeing with him, are you? [*She comes forward and puts her arm about his shoulder – with a determined gaiety.*] Aw say, what's the matter? Cut out the gloom. We're all fixed now, ain't we, me and you? [*Pours out more beer into his glass and fills one for herself – slaps him on the back.*] Come on! Here's to the sea, no matter what! Be a game sport and drink to that! Come on!

[*She gulps down her glass.* BURKE *banishes his superstitious premonitions with a defiant jerk of his head, grins up at her, and drinks to her toast.*]

CHRIS [*looking out into the night – lost in his sombre preoccupation – shakes his head and mutters*]: Fog, fog, fog, all bloody time. You can't see vhere you vas going, no. Only dat ole davil, sea – she knows! [*The two stare at him. From the harbour comes the muffled, mournful wail of steamers' whistles.*]

THE CURTAIN FALLS

THE EMPEROR JONES

CHARACTERS

BRUTUS JONES, Emperor

HENRY SMITHERS, A Cockney Trader

AN OLD NATIVE WOMAN

LEM, A Native Chief

SOLDIERS, Adherents of Lem

The Little Formless Fears; Jeff; the Negro Convicts; the
Prison Guard; the Planters; the Auctioneer; the
Slaves; the Congo Witch-Doctor; the Crocodile
God

The action of the play takes place on an island in the
West Indies as yet not self-determined by White Mariners.
The form of native government is, for the time being, an
Empire

SCENE ONE

*The audience chamber in the palace of the Emperor – a spacious,
high-ceilinged room with bare, whitewashed walls. The floor is
of white tiles. In the rear, to the left of centre, a wide archway giving
out on a portico with white pillars. The palace is evidently situated
on high ground, for beyond the portico nothing can be seen but a vista
of distant hills, their summits crowned with thick groves of palm
trees. In the right wall, centre, a smaller arched doorway leading
to the living quarters of the palace. The room is bare of furniture
with the exception of one huge chair made of uncut wood which
stands at centre, its back to rear. This is very apparently the
Emperor's throne. It is painted a dazzling, eye-smiting scarlet.
There is a brilliant orange cushion on the seat and another smaller
one is placed on the floor to serve as a footstool. Strips of matting,
dyed scarlet, lead from the foot of the throne to the two entrances.*

*It is late afternoon, but the yellow sunlight still blazes beyond
the portico and there is an oppressive burden of exhausting heat in
the air.*

[*As the curtain rises, a native* NEGRO WOMAN *sneaks in
cautiously from the entrance on the right. She is very old,
dressed in cheap calico, bare-footed, a red bandana handkerchief covering all but a few stray wisps of white hair. A bundle
bound in coloured cloth is carried over her shoulder on the end
of a stick. She hesitates beside the doorway, peering back as if
in extreme dread of being discovered. Then she begins to glide
noiselessly, a step at a time, towards the doorway in the rear.
At this moment* SMITHERS *appears beneath the portico.*

SMITHERS *is a tall man, round-shouldered, about forty.
His bald head, perched on a long neck with an enormous
Adam's apple, looks like an egg. The tropics have tanned his
naturally pasty face with its small, sharp features to a sickly
yellow, and native rum has painted his pointed nose to a*

*startling red. His little washy-blue eyes are red-rimmed and
dart about him like a ferret's. His expression is one of un-
scrupulous meanness, cowardly and dangerous. He is dressed
in a worn riding suit of dirty white drill, puttees, and spurs, and
wears a white cork helmet. A cartridge belt with an automatic
revolver is around his waist. He carries a riding whip in his
hand. He sees the woman and stops to watch her suspiciously.
Then, making up his mind, he steps quickly on tiptoe into the
room. The* WOMAN, *looking back over her shoulder continually, does not see him until it is too late. When she does*
SMITHERS *springs forward and grabs her firmly by the
shoulder. She struggles to get away, fiercely but silently.*]

SMITHERS [*tightening his grasp – roughly*]: Easy! None o' that,
me birdie. You can't wriggle out now. I got me 'ooks on
yer.

WOMAN [*seeing the uselessness of struggling, gives way to frantic
terror, and sinks to the ground, embracing his knees supplicatingly*]: No tell him! No tell him, Mister!

SMITHERS [*with great curiosity*]: Tell 'im? [*Then scornfully*] Oh,
you mean 'is bloomin' Majesty. What's the game, any 'ow?
What are you sneakin' away for? Been stealin' a bit, I
s'pose. [*He taps her bundle with his riding whip significantly.*]

WOMAN [*shaking her head vehemently*]: No, me no steal.

SMITHERS: Bloody liar! But tell me what's up. There's
somethin' funny goin' on. I smelled it in the air first thing I
got up this mornin'. You blacks are up to some devilment.
This palace of 'is is like a bleedin' tomb. Where's all the
'ands? [*The* WOMAN *keeps sullenly silent.* SMITHERS *raises his
whip threateningly.*] Ow, yer won't, won't yer? I'll show yer
what's what.

WOMAN [*coweringly*]: I tell, Mister. You no hit. They go – all
go. [*She makes a sweeping gesture towards the hills in the
distance.*]

SMITHERS: Run away – to the 'ills?

WOMAN: Yes, Mister. Him Emperor – Great Father. [*She touches her forehead to the floor with a quick mechanical jerk.*] Him sleep after eat. Then they go – all go. Me old woman. Me left only. Now me go too.

SMITHERS [*his astonishment giving way to an immense, mean satisfaction*]: Ow! So that's the ticket! Well, I know bloody well wot's in the air – when they runs orf to the 'ills. The tom-tom'll be thumping out there bloomin' soon. [*With extreme vindictiveness*] And I'm bloody glad of it, for one! Serve 'im right! Puttin' on airs, the stinkin' nigger! 'Is Majesty! Gawd blimey! I only 'opes I'm there when they takes 'im out to shoot 'im. [*Suddenly*] 'E's still 'ere all right, ain't 'e?

WOMAN: Yes. Him sleep.

SMITHERS: 'E's bound to find out soon as 'e wakes up. 'E's cunnin' enough to know when 'is time's come. [*He goes to the doorway on right and whistles shrilly with his fingers in his mouth. The* OLD WOMAN *springs to her feet and runs out of the doorway, rear.* SMITHERS *goes after her, reaching for his revolver.*] Stop or I'll shoot! [*Then stopping – indifferently*] Pop orf then, if yer like, yer black cow. [*He stands in the doorway, looking after her.*]

[JONES *enters from the right. He is a tall, powerfully built, full-blooded Negro of middle age. His features are typically negroid, yet there is something decidedly distinctive about his face – an underlying strength of will, a hardy, self-reliant confidence in himself that inspires respect. His eyes are alive with a keen, cunning intelligence. In manner he is shrewd, suspicious, evasive. He wears a light blue uniform coat, sprayed with brass buttons, heavy gold chevrons on his shoulders, gold braid on the collar, cuffs, etc. His trousers are bright red with a light blue stripe down the side. Patent-leather laced boots with brass spurs, and a belt with a long-barrelled, pearl-handled revolver in a holster complete his attire. Yet there is something not altogether ridiculous about his grandeur. He has a way of carrying it off.*]

JONES [*not seeing anyone – greatly irritated and blinking sleepily – shouts*]: Who dare whistle dat way in my palace? Who dare wake up de Emperor? I'll git de hide flayed off some o' you niggers sho'!

SMITHERS [*showing himself – in a manner half-afraid and half-defiant*]: It was me whistled to yer. [*As* JONES *frowns angrily*] I got news for yer.

JONES [*putting on his suavest manner, which fails to cover up his contempt for the white man*]: Oh, it's you, Mister Smithers. [*He sits down on his throne with easy dignity.*] What news you got to tell me?

SMITHERS [*coming close to enjoy his discomfiture*]: Don't yer notice nothin' funny today?

JONES [*coldly*]: Funny? No. I ain't perceived nothin' of de kind!

SMITHERS: Then yer ain't so foxy as I thought yer was. Where's all your court? [*Sarcastically*] The Generals and the Cabinet Ministers and all?

JONES [*imperturbably*]: Where dey mostly runs to minute I closes my eyes – drinkin' rum and talkin' big down in de town. [*Sarcastically*] How come you don't know dat? Ain't you carousing with 'em most every day?

SMITHERS [*stung, but pretending indifference – with a wink*]: That's part of the day's work. I got ter – ain't I – in my business?

JONES [*contemptuously*]: Yo' business!

SMITHERS [*imprudently enraged*]: Gawd blimey, you was glad enough for me ter take yer in on it when you landed 'ere first. You didn't 'ave no 'igh and mighty airs in them days!

JONES [*his hand going to his revolver like a flash – menacingly*]: Talk polite, white man! Talk polite, you heah me! I'm boss heah now, is you fergettin'?

[*The Cockney seems about to challenge this last statement with the facts, but something in the other's eyes holds and cows him.*]

SMITHERS [*in a cowardly whine*]: No 'arm meant, old top.

JONES [*condescendingly*]: I accepts yo' apology. [*Lets his hand fall from his revolver.*] No use'n you rakin' up ole times. What I was den is one thing. What I is now 's another. You didn't let me in on yo' crooked work out o' no kind feelin's dat time. I done de dirty work fo' you – and most o' de brain work, too, fo' dat matter – and I was wu'th money to you, dat's de reason.

SMITHERS: Well, blimey, I give yer a start, didn't I – when no one else would. I wasn't afraid to 'ire yer like the rest was – 'count of the story about your breakin' jail back in the States.

JONES: No, you didn't have no s'cuse to look down on me fo' dat. You been in jail you'self more'n once.

SMITHERS [*furiously*]: It's a lie! [*Then trying to pass it off by an attempt at scorn.*] Garn! Who told yer that fairy tale?

JONES: Dey's some tings I ain't got to be tole. I kin see 'em in folk's eyes. [*Then after a pause – meditatively*] Yes, you sho' give me a start. And it didn't take long from dat time to git dese fool woods' niggers right where I wanted dem. [*With pride*] From stowaway to Emperor in two years! Dat's goin' some!

SMITHERS [*with curiosity*]: And I bet you got yer pile o' money 'id safe some place.

JONES [*with satisfaction*]: I sho' has! And it's in a foreign bank where no pusson don't ever git it out but me no matter what come. You didn't s'pose I was holdin' down dis Emperor job for de glory in it, did you? Sho'! De fuss and glory part of it, dat's only to turn de heads o' de low-flung bush niggers dat's here. Dey wants de big circus show for deir money. I gives it to 'em an' I gits de money. [*With a grin*] De long green, dat's me every time! [*Then rebukingly*] But you ain't got no kick agin me, Smithers. I'se paid you back all you done for me many times. Ain't I pertected you and winked at all de crooked tradin' you been doin' right out in de broad day. Sho' I has – and me makin' laws to stop it at de same time! [*He chuckles.*]

SMITHERS [*grinning*]: But, meanin' no 'arm, you been grabbin' right and left yourself, ain't yer! Look at the taxes you've put on 'em! Blimey! You've squeezed 'em dry!

JONES [*chuckling*]: No, dey ain't *all* dry yet. I'se still heah, ain't I?

SMITHERS [*smiling at his secret thought*]: They're dry right now, you'll find out. [*Changing the subject abruptly*] And as for me breakin' laws, you've broke 'em all yerself just as fast as yer made 'em.

JONES: Ain't I de Emperor? De laws don't go for him. [*Judicially*] You heah what I tells you, Smithers. Dere's little stealin' like you does, and dere's big stealin' like I does. For de little stealin' dey gits you in jail soon or late. For de big stealin' dey makes you Emperor and puts you in de Hall o' Fame when you croaks. [*Reminiscently*] If dey's one thing I learns in ten years on de Pullman ca's listenin' to de white quality talk, it's dat same fact. And when I gits a chance to use it I winds up Emperor in two years.

SMITHERS [*unable to repress the genuine admiration of the small fry for the large*]: Yes, yer turned the bleedin' trick, all right. Blimey, I never seen a bloke 'as 'ad the bloomin' luck you 'as.

JONES [*severely*]: Luck? What you mean – luck?

SMITHERS: I suppose you'll say as that swank about the silver bullet ain't luck – and that was what first got the fool blacks on yer side the time of the revolution, wasn't it?

JONES [*with a laugh*]: Oh, dat silver bullet! Sho' was luck! But I makes dat luck, you heah? I loads de dice! Yessuh! When dat murderin' nigger ole Lem hired to kill me takes aim ten feet away and his gun misses fire and I shoots him dead, what you heah me say?

SMITHERS: You said yer'd got a charm so's no lead bullet'd kill yer. You was so strong only a silver bullet could kill yer, you told 'em. Blimey, wasn't that swank for yer, and plain, fat-'eaded luck?

JONES [*proudly*]: I got brains and I uses 'em quick. Dat ain't luck.

SMITHERS: Yer know they wasn't 'ardly liable to get no silver bullets. And it was luck 'e didn't 'it you that time.

JONES [*laughing*]: And dere all dem fool bush niggers was kneelin' down and bumpin' deir heads on de ground like I was a miracle out o' de Bible. Oh Lawd, from dat time on I has dem all eatin' out of my hand. I cracks de whip and dey jumps through.

SMITHERS [*with a sniff*]: Yankee bluff done it.

JONES: Ain't a man's talkin' big what makes him big – long as he makes folks believe it? Sho', I talks large when I ain't got nothin' to back it up, but I ain't talkin' wild just de same. I knows I kin fool 'em – I *knows* it – and dat's backin' enough fo' my game. And ain't I got to learn deir lingo and teach some of dem English befo' I kin talk to em? Ain't dat wuk? You ain't never learned any word of it, Smithers, in de ten years you been heah, dough you knows it's money in yo' pocket tradin' wid 'em if you does. But you'se too shiftless to take de trouble.

SMITHERS [*flushing*]: Never mind about me. What's this I've 'eard about yer really 'avin' a silver bullet moulded for yourself?

JONES: It's playin' out my bluff. I has de silver bullet moulded and I tells 'em when de time comes I kills myself wid it. I tells 'em dat's 'cause I'm de on'y man in de world big enuff to git me. No use'n deir tryin'. And dey falls down and bumps deir heads. [*He laughs.*] I does dat so's I kin take a walk in peace widout no jealous nigger gunnin' at me from behind de trees.

SMITHERS [*astonished*]: Then you 'ad it made – 'onest?

JONES: Sho' did. Heah she be. [*He takes out his revolver, breaks it, and takes the bullet out of one chamber.*] Five lead an' dis silver baby at de last. Don't she shine pretty? [*He holds it in his hand, looking at it admiringly, as if strangely fascinated.*]

SMITHERS: Let me see. [*Reaches out his hand for it.*]

JONES [*harshly*]: Keep yo' hands whar dey b'long, white man [*He replaces it in the chamber and puts the revolver back on his hip.*]

SMITHERS [*snarling*]: Gawd blimey! Think I'm a bleedin' thief, you would.

JONES: No, 'tain't dat. I knows you'se scared to steal from me. On'y I ain't 'lowin' nary body to touch dis baby. She's my rabbit's foot.

SMITHERS [*sneering*]: A bloomin' charm, wot? [*Venomously*] Well, you'll need all the bloody charms you 'as before long, s' 'elp me!

JONES [*judicially*]: Oh, I'se good for six months yit 'fore dey gits sick o' my game. Den, when I sees trouble comin', I makes a move.

SMITHERS: Ho! You got it all planned, ain't yer?

JONES: I ain't no fool. I know dis Emperor's time is sho't. Dat why I make hay when de sun shine. Was you thinkin' I'se aimin' to hold down dis job for life? No, suh! What good is gittin' money if you stays back in dis raggedy country? I wants action when I spends. And when I sees dese niggers gittin' up deir nerve to tu'n me out, and I'se got all de money in sight, I resigns on de spot and gets away quick.

SMITHERS: Where to?

JONES: None o' yo' business.

SMITHERS: Not back to the bloody States, I'll lay my oath.

JONES [*suspiciously*]: Why don't I? [*Then with an easy laugh*] You mean 'count of dat story 'bout me breakin' from jail back dere? Dat's all talk.

SMITHERS [*sceptically*]: Ho, yes!

JONES [*sharply*]: You ain't 'sinuatin' I'se a liar, is you?

SMITHERS [*hastily*]: No, Gawd strike me! I was only thinkin' o' the bloody lies you told the blacks 'ere about killin' white men in the States.

JONES [*angered*]: How come dey're lies?

SMITHERS: You'd 'ave been in jail if you 'ad, wouldn't yer then? [*With venom*] And from what I've 'eard, it ain't 'ealthy for a black to kill a white man in the States. They burns 'em in oil, don't they?

JONES [*with cool deadliness*]: You mean lynchin' 'd scare me? Well, I tells you, Smithers, maybe I does kill one white man back dere. Maybe I does. And maybe I kills another right heah 'fore long if he don't look out.

SMITHERS [*trying to force a laugh*]: I was on'y spoofin' yer. Can't yer take a joke? And you was just sayin' you'd never been in jail.

JONES [*in the same tone – slightly boastful*]: Maybe I goes to jail dere for gettin' in an argument wid razors ovah a game of dice. Maybe I gits twenty years when dat coloured man die. Maybe I gits in 'nother argument wid de prison guard and de overseer ovah us when we're wukin' de roads. Maybe he hits me wid a whip and I splits his head wid a shovel and runs away and files de chain off my leg and gits away safe. Maybe I does all dat an' maybe I don't. It's a story I tells you so's you knows I'se de kind of man dat if you evah repeats one word of it, I ends yo' stealin' on dis yearth mighty damn quick!

SMITHERS [*terrified*]: Think I'd peach on yer? Not me! Ain't I always been yer friend?

JONES [*suddenly relaxing*]: Sho' you has – and you better be.

SMITHERS [*recovering his composure – and with it his malice*]: And just to show yer I'm yer friend, I'll tell yer that bit o' news I was goin' to.

JONES: Go ahead! Must be bad news from de happy way you look.

SMITHERS [*warningly*]: Maybe it's gettin' time for you to

resign – with that bloomin' silver bullet, wot? [*He finishes with a mocking grin.*]

JONES [*puzzled*]: What's dat you say? Talk plain.

SMITHERS: Ain't noticed any of the guards or servants about the place today, I 'aven't.

JONES [*carelessly*]: Dey're all out in de garden sleepin' under de trees. When I sleeps, dey sneaks a sleep too, and I pretends I never suspicions it. All I got to do is to ring de bell and dey come flyin', makin' a bluff dey was wukin' all de time.

SMITHERS [*in the same mocking tone*]: Ring the bell now an' you'll bloody well see what I mean.

JONES [*startled to alertness, but preserving the same careless tone*]: Sho' I rings.

[*He reaches below the throne and pulls out a big common dinner bell which is painted the same vivid scarlet as the throne. He rings this vigorously – then stops to listen. Then he goes to both doors, rings again, and looks out.*]

SMITHERS [*watching him with malicious satisfaction, after a pause – mockingly*]: The bloody ship is sinkin' an' the bleedin' rats 'as slung their 'ooks.

JONES [*in a sudden fit of anger flings the bell clattering into a corner*]: Low-flung bush niggers! [*Then catching* SMITHERS' *eye on him, he controls himself and suddenly bursts into a low chuckling laugh.*] Reckon I overplays my hand dis once! A man can't take de pot on a short-tailed flush all de time. Was I sayin' I'd sit it six months mo'? Well, I'se changed my mind den. I gives in and resigns de job of Emperor right dis minute.

SMITHERS [*with real admiration*]: Blimey, but you're a cool bird, and no mistake.

JONES: No use'n fussin'. When I knows de game's up I kisses it good-bye widout no long waits. Dey've all run off to de hills, ain't dey?

SMITHERS: Yes – every bleedin' man jack of 'em.

JONES: Den de revolution is at de door. And de Emperor better git his feet movin' up de trail. [*He starts for the door in rear.*]

SMITHERS: Goin' out to look for your 'orse? Yer won't find any. They steals the 'orses first thing. Mine was gone when I went for 'im this mornin'. That's wot first give me a suspicion of wot was up.

JONES [*alarmed for a second, scratches his head, then philosophically*]: Well, den I hoofs it. Feet, do yo' duty! [*He pulls out a gold watch and looks at it.*] Three-thuty. Sundown's at six-thuty or dereabouts. [*Puts his watch back – with cool confidence.*] I got plenty o' time to make it easy.

SMITHERS: Don't be so bloomin' sure of it. They'll be after you 'ot and 'eavy. Ole Lem is at the bottom o' this business an' 'e 'ates you like 'ell. 'E'd rather do for you than eat 'is dinner, 'e would!

JONES [*scornfully*]: Dat fool no-count nigger! Does you think I'se scared o' him? I stands him on his thick head more'n once befo' dis, and I does it again if he comes in my way – [*Fiercely*] And dis time I leave him a dead nigger fo' sho'!

SMITHERS: You'll 'ave to cut through the big forest – an' these blacks 'ere can sniff and follow a trail in the dark like 'ounds. You'd 'ave to 'ustle to get through that forest in twelve hours even if you knew all the bloomin' paths like a native.

JONES [*with indignant scorn*]: Look-a-heah, white man! Does you think I'se a natural bo'n fool? Give me credit fo' havin' some sense, fo' Lawd's sake! Don't you s'pose I'se looked ahead and made sho' of all de chances? I'se gone out in dat big forest, pretendin' to hunt, so many times dat I knows it high an' low like a book. I could go through on dem paths wid my eyes shut. [*With great contempt*] Think dese ig'nerent bush niggers dat ain't got brains enuff to know deir own names even, can catch Brutus Jones? Huh, I s'pects not! Not on yo' life! Why, man, de white men went after me wid bloodhounds, where I come from an' I jes' laughs at 'em. It's a shame to fool dese black trash around heah, dey're so easy. You watch me, man. I'll make dem look sick, I will. I'll be 'cross de plain to de edge of de forest by time dark comes. Once in de woods in de night, dey got a fine chance o' findin' dis baby! Dawn tomorrow I'll be out at de oder side and on de coast whar dat French gunboat is stayin'. She picks me up, take me to the Martinique when she go dar, and dere I is safe wid a mighty big bankroll in my pocket. It's easy as rollin' off a log.

SMITHERS [*maliciously*]: But s'posin' somethin' 'appens wrong an' they do nab yer?

JONES [*decisively*]: Dey don't – dat's de answer.

SMITHERS: But, just for argyment's sake – what'd you do?

JONES [*frowning*]: I'se got five lead bullets in dis gun good enuff fo' common bush niggers – and after dat I got de silver bullet left to cheat 'em out o' gittin' me.

SMITHERS [*jeeringly*]: Ho, I was fergettin' that silver bullet. You'll bump yourself orf in style, won't yer? Blimey!

JONES [*gloomily*]: You kin bet yo' whole money on one thing, white man. Dis baby plays out his string to de end and when he quits, he quits wid a bang de way he ought. Silver bullet ain't none too good for him when he go, dat's a fac'! [*Then shaking off his nervousness – with a confident laugh.*] Sho'! What is I talkin' about? Ain't come to dat yit and I never will – not wid trash niggers like dese yere. [*Boastfully*] Silver bullet bring me luck anyway. I kin outguess, outrun, outfight, an' outplay de whole lot o' dem all ovah de board any time o' de day er night! You watch me!

[*From the distant hills comes the faint, steady thump of a tom-tom, low and vibrating. It starts at a rate exactly corresponding to normal pulse beat – seventy-two to the minute – and continues at a gradually accelerating rate from this point uninterruptedly to the very end of the play.*]

JONES [*starts at the sound. A strange look of apprehension creeps into his face for a moment as he listens. Then he asks, with an attempt to regain his most casual manner*]: What's dat drum beatin' fo'?

SMITHERS [*with a mean grin*]: For you. That means the bleedin' ceremony 'as started. I've 'eard it before and I knows.

JONES: Cer'mony? What cer'mony?

SMITHERS: The blacks is 'oldin' a bloody meetin', 'avin' a war dance, gettin' their courage worked up b'fore they starts after you.

JONES: Let dem! Dey'll sho' need it!

SMITHERS: And they're there 'oldin' their 'eathen religious service – makin' no end of devil spells and charms to 'elp 'em against your silver bullet. [*He guffaws loudly.*] Blimey, but they're balmy as 'ell!

JONES [*a tiny bit awed and shaken in spite of himself*]: Huh! Takes more'n dat to scare dis chicken!

SMITHERS [*scenting the other's feeling – maliciously*]: Ternight when it's pitch black in the forest, they'll 'ave their pet devils and ghosts 'oundin' after you. You'll find yer bloody 'air 'll be standin' on end before termorrow mornin'. [*Seriously*] It's a bleedin' queer place, that stinkin' forest, even in daylight. Yer don't know what might 'appen in there, it's that rotten still. Always sends the cold shivers down my back minute I gets in it.

JONES [*with a contemptuous sniff*]: I ain't no white-liver like you is. Trees an' me, we'se friends, and dar's a full moon comin' bring me light. And let dem po' niggers make all de fool spells dey'se a min' to. Does yo' s'pect I'se silly enuff to b'lieve in ghosts an' ha'nts an' all dat ole woman's talk? G'long, white man! You ain't talkin' to me. [*With a chuckle*] Doesn't you know dey's got to do wid a man who was member in good standin' o' de Baptist Church? Sho' I was dat when I was porter on de Pullmans, befo' I gits into my little trouble. Let dem try deir heathen tricks. De Baptist Church done pertect me and land dem all in hell. [*Then with more confident satisfaction*] And I'se got little silver bullet o' my own, don't forgit.

SMITHERS: Ho! You 'aven't give much 'eed to your Baptist Church since you been down 'ere. I've 'eard myself you 'ad turned yer coat an' was takin' up with their blarsted witch-doctors, or whatever the 'ell yer calls the swine.

JONES [*vehemently*]: I pretends to! Sho' I pretends! Dat's part o' my game from de fust. If I finds out dem niggers believes dat black is white, den I yells it out louder 'n deir loudest. It don't git me nothin' to do missionary work for de Baptist Church. I'se after de coin, an' I lays my Jesus on de shelf for de time bein'. [*Stops abruptly to look at his watch – alertly.*] But I ain't got de time to waste no more fool talk wid you. I'se gwine away from heah dis secon'. [*He reaches in under the throne and pulls out an expensive Panama hat with a bright multi-coloured band and sets it jauntily on his head.*] So long, white man! [*With a grin*] See you in jail some time, maybe!

SMITHERS: Not me, you won't. Well, I wouldn't be in yer bloody boots for no bloomin' money, but 'ere's wishin' yer luck just the same.

JONES [*contemptuously*]: You're de frightenedest man evah I see! I tells you I'se safe's 'f I was in New York City. It takes dem niggers from now to dark to git up de nerve to start somethin'. By dat time, I'se got a head start dey never kotch up wid.

SMITHERS [*maliciously*]: Give my regards to any ghosts yer meets up with.

JONES [*grinning*]: If dat ghost got money, I'll tell him never ha'nt you less'n he wants to lose it.

SMITHERS [*flattered*]: Garn! [*Then curiously*] Ain't yer takin' no luggage with yer?

JONES: I travels light when I wants to move fast. And I got tinned grub buried on de edge o' de forest. [*Boastfully*] Now say dat I don't look ahead an' use my brains! [*With a wide, liberal gesture*] I will all dat's left in de palace to you – and you better grab all you kin sneak away wid befo' dey gits here.

SMITHERS [*gratefully*]: Righto – and thanks ter yer. [*As* JONES *walks towards the door in rear – cautioningly*] Say! Look 'ere, you ain't goin' out that way, are yer?

JONES: Does you think I'd slink out de back door like a common nigger? I'se Emperor yit, ain't I? And de Emperor Jones leaves de way he comes, and dat black trash don't dare stop him – not yit, leastways. [*He stops for a moment in the doorway, listening to the far-off but insistent beat of the tom-tom.*] Listen to dat roll-call, will you? Must be mighty big drum carry dat far. [*Then with a laugh*] Well, if dey ain't no whole brass band to see me off, I sho' got de drum part of it. So long, white man.

[*He puts his hands in his pockets and with studied carelessness, whistling a tune, he saunters out of the doorway and off to left.*]

SMITHERS [*looks after him with a puzzled admiration*]: 'E's got 'is bloomin' nerve with 'im, s'elp me! [*Then angrily*] Ho – the bleedin' nigger – puttin' on 'is bloody airs! I 'opes they nabs 'im an' gives 'im what's what! [*Then putting business before the pleasure of this thought, looking around him with cupidity*] A bloke ought to find a 'ole lot in this palace that'd go for a bit of cash. Let's take a look, 'Arry, me lad.

[*He starts for the doorway on right as the curtain falls.*]

SCENE TWO

NIGHTFALL

The end of the plain where the Great Forest begins. The foreground is sandy, level ground dotted by a few stones and clumps of stunted bushes cowering close against the earth to escape the buffeting of the trade wind. In the rear the forest is a wall of darkness dividing the world. Only when the eye becomes accustomed to the gloom can the outlines of separate trunks of the nearest trees be made out, enormous pillars of deeper blackness. A sombre monotone of wind lost in the leaves moans in the air. Yet this sound serves but to intensify the impression of the forest's relentless immobility, to form a background throwing into relief its brooding, implacable silence.

> [JONES *enters from the left, walking rapidly. He stops as he nears the edge of the forest, looks around him quickly, peering into the dark as if searching for some familiar landmark. Then, apparently satisfied that he is where he ought to be, he throws himself on the ground, dog-tired.*]

JONES: Well, heah I is. In de nick o' time, too! Little mo' an' it'd be blacker'n de ace of spades heah-abouts. [*He pulls a bandana handkerchief from his hip pocket and mops off his perspiring face.*] Sho'! Gimme air! I'se done up sho' 'nuff. Dat soft Emperor job ain't no trainin' fo' a long dash ovah dat plain in de brilin' sun. [*Then with a chuckle*] Cheah up, nigger, de worst is yet to come. [*He lifts his head and stares at the forest. His chuckle peters out abruptly. In a tone of awe*] My goodness, look at dem woods, will you? Dat no-count Smithers said dey'd be black an' he sho' called de turn. [*Turning away from them quickly and looking down at his feet, he snatches at a chance to change the subject – solicitously.*] Feet, you is holdin' up yo' end fine an' I sutinly hopes you ain't blisterin'. It's time you git a rest. [*He takes off his shoes, his eyes studiously avoiding the forest. He feels the soles of his feet gingerly.*] You is still in de pink – on'y a little mite feverish. Cool yo'selfs. Remember you got a long journey yit before you. [*He sits in a weary attitude, listening to the rhythmic beating of the tom-tom. He grumbles in a loud tone to cover up a growing uneasiness.*] Bush niggers! Wonder dey wouldn' git sick o' beatin' dat drum. Sounds louder, seem like. I wonder if dey's startin' after me? [*He scrambles to his feet, looking back across the plain.*] Couldn't see dem now, nohow, if dey was hundred feet away. [*Then shaking himself like a wet dog to get rid of these depressing thoughts*] Sho', dey's miles an' miles behind. What you gittin' fidgety about? [*But he sits down and begins to lace up his shoes in great haste, all the time muttering reassuringly.*] You know what? Yo' belly is empty, dat's what's de matter wid you. Come time to eat! Wid nothin' but wind on yo' stumach, o' course you feels jiggedy. Well, we eats right heah an' now soon's I gits dese here shoes laced up. [*He finishes lacing up his shoes.*] Dere! Now le's see! [*Gets on his hands and knees and searches the ground around him with his eyes.*] White stone, white stone, where is you? [*He sees the first white stone and crawls to it – with satisfaction.*] Heah you is! I knowed dis was de right place. Box of grub, come to me. [*He turns over the stone and feels in under it – in a tone of dismay.*] Ain't heah! Gorry, is I in de right place or isn't I? Dere's 'nother stone. Guess dat's it. [*He scrambles to the next stone and turns it over.*] Ain't heah, neither! Grub, whar is you? Ain't heah. Gorry, has I got to go hungry into dem woods – all de night? [*While he is talking he scrambles from one stone to another, turning them over in frantic haste. Finally he jumps to his feet excitedly.*] Is I lost de place? Must have! But how dat happen when I was followin' de trail across de plain in broad daylight? [*Almost plaintively*] I'se hungry, I is! I gotta git my feed. Whar's my strength gonna come from if I doesn't? Gorry, I gotta find dat grub high an' low somehow! Why it come dark so quick like dat? Can't see nothin'. [*He scratches a match on his trousers and peers about him. The rate of the beat of the far-off tom-tom increases perceptibly as he does so. He mutters in a bewildered voice.*] How come all dese white stones come heah when I only remembers one? [*Suddenly, with a frightened gasp, he flings the match on the ground and stamps on it.*] Nigger, is you gone crazy mad? Is you lightin' matches to show dem whar you is? Fo' Lawd's sake, use yo' haid. Gorry, I'se got to be careful! [*He stares at the plain behind him apprehensively, his hand on his revolver.*] But how come all dese white stones? And whar's dat tin box o' grub I hid all wrapped up in oil cloth?

[*While his back is turned, the* LITTLE FORMLESS FEARS *creep out from the deeper blackness of the forest. They are black, shapeless, only their glittering little eyes can be seen. If they have any describable form at all it is that of a grubworm about the size of a creeping child. They move noiselessly, but with deliberate, painful effort, striving to raise themselves on end, failing and sinking prone again.* JONES *turns about to face the forest. He stares up at the tops of the trees, seeking vainly to discover his whereabout by their conformation.*]

JONES: Can't tell nothin' from dem trees! Gorry, nothin' 'round heah look like I evah seed it befo'. I'se gone lost de place sho' 'nuff. [*With mournful foreboding*] It's mighty queer! It's mighty queer! [*With sudden forced defiance – in an angry tone*] Woods, is you tryin' to put somethin' ovah on me? [*From the formless creatures on the ground in front of him comes a tiny gale of low mocking laughter like a rustling of leaves. They squirm upward towards him in twisted attitudes.* JONES *looks down, leaps backwards with a yell of terror, pulling out his revolver as he does so—in a quavering voice.*] What's dat? Who's dar? What is you? Git away from me befo' I shoots! You don't? –

[*He fires. There is a flash, a loud report, then silence broken only by the far-off quickened throb of the tom-tom. The form-less creatures have scurried back into the forest.* JONES *remains fixed in his position listening intently. The sound of the shot, the reassuring feel of the revolver in his hand, have some-what restored his shaken nerve. He addresses himself with renewed confidence.*]

JONES: Dey're gone. Dat shot fix 'em. Dey was only little animals – little wild pigs, I reckon. Dey've maybe rooted out yo' grub an' eat it. Sho', you fool nigger, what you think dey is – ha'nts. [*Excitedly*] Gorry, you give de game away when you fire dat shot. Dem niggers heah dat fo' su'tin! Time you beat it in de woods widout no long waits. [*He starts for the forest – hesitates before the plunge – then urging himself in with manful resolution.*] Git in, nigger! What you skeered at? Ain't nothin' dere but de trees! Git in! [*He plunges boldly into the forest.*]

SCENE THREE

Nine o'clock. In the forest. The moon has just risen. Its beams, drifting through the canopy of leaves, make a barely perceptible, suffused, eerie glow. A dense low wall of underbrush and creepers is in the nearer forground, fencing in a small triangular clearing. Beyond this is the massed blackness of the forest like an encompassing barrier. A path is dimly discerned leading down to the clearing from left, rear, and winding away from it again towards the right.

[As the scene opens nothing can be distinctly made out. Except for the beating of the tom-tom, which is a trifle louder and quicker than in the previous scene, there is silence, broken every few seconds by a queer, clicking sound. Then gradually the figure of the Negro, JEFF, can be discerned crouching on his haunches at the rear of the triangle He is middle-aged, thin, brown in colour, is dressed in a Pullman porter's uniform, cap, etc. He is throwing a pair of dice on the ground before him, picking them up, shaking them, casting them out with the regular, rigid, mechanical movements of an automaton. The heavy, plodding footsteps of someone approaching along the trail from the left are heard and JONES's voice, pitched in a slightly higher key and strained in a cheering effort to overcome its own tremors.]

JONES: De moon's rizen. Does you heah dat, nigger? You gits more light from dis forrard. No mo' buttin' yo' fool head agin' de trunks an' scratchin' de hide off yo' legs in de bushes. Now you sees whar you'se gwine. So cheer up! From now on you has it easy. [He steps just to the rear of the triangular clearing and mops off his face on his sleeve. He has lost his Panama hat. His face is scratched, his brilliant uniform shows several large rents.] What time's it gittin' to be, I wonder? I dassent light no match to find out. Phoo'. It's wa'm an' dat's a fac'! [*Wearily*] How long I been makin' trampin' dese woods? Must be hours an' hours. Seems like fo'evah! Yit can't be, when de moon's jes' riz. Dis am a long night fo' yo', yo' Majesty! [*With a mournful chuckle*] Majesty! Der ain't much majesty 'bout dis baby now. [*With attempted cheerfulness*] Never min'. It's all part o' de game. Dis night come to an end like everything else. And when you gits dar safe and has dat bankroll in yo' hands you laughs at all dis. [*He starts to whistle, but checks himself abruptly.*] What yo' whistlin' for, you po' fool! Want all de worl' to heah you? [*He stops talking to listen.*] Heah dat ole drum! Sho' gits nearer from de sound. Dey're takin' it along wid 'em. Time fo' me to move. [*He takes a step forward, then stops — worriedly.*] What's dat odder queer clickety sound I heah? Dere it is! Sound close! Sound like — sound like — Fo' God sake, sound like some nigger was shootin' dice! [*Frightenedly*] I better get on quick when I gits dem notions. [*He walks quickly into the clear space — then stands transfixed as he sees* JEFF — *in a terrified gasp*] Who dar? Who dat? Is dat you, Jeff? [*Starting towards the other, forgetful for a moment of his surroundings and really believing it is a living man that he sees — in a tone of happy relief.*] Jeff! I'se sho' mighty glad to see you! Dey tol' me you done died from dat razor cut I give you. [*Stopping suddenly, bewildered*] But how you come to be heah, nigger? [*He stares fascinatedly at the other who continues his mechanical play with the dice.* JONES'S *eyes begin to roll wildly. He stutters.*] Ain't you gwine — look up — can't you speak to me? Is you — is you — a ha'nt? [*He jerks out his revolver in a frenzy of terrified rage.*] Nigger, I kills you dead once. Has I got to kill you agin? You take it den. [*He fires. When the smoke clears away* JEFF *has disappeared.* JONES *stands trembling — then with a certain reassurance.*] He's gone, anyway. Ha'nt or no ha'nt, dat shot fix him. [*The beat of the far-off tom-tom is perceptibly louder and more rapid.* JONES *becomes conscious of it — with a start, looking back over his shoulder.*] Dey's gittin' near! Dey'se comin' fast! And heah I is shootin' shots to let 'em know jes' whar I is. Oh, Gorry, I'se got to run. [*Forgetting the path he plunges wildly into the underbrush in the rear and disappears in the shadow.*]

SCENE FOUR

Eleven o'clock. In the forest. A wide dirt road runs diagonally from right, front, to left, rear. Rising sheer on both sides the forest walls it in. The moon is now up. Under its light the road glimmers ghastly and unreal. It is as if the forest has stood aside momentarily to let the road pass through and accomplish its veiled purpose. This done, the forest will fold in upon itself again and the road will be no more.

[JONES stumbles in from the forest on the right. His uniform is ragged and torn. He looks about him with numbed surprise when he sees the road, his eyes blinking in the bright moonlight. He flops down exhaustedly and pants heavily for a while. Then with sudden anger.]

JONES: I'm meltin' wid heat! Runnin' an' runnin' an' runnin'! Damn dis heah coat! Like a strait-jacket! *[He tears off his coat and flings it away from him, revealing himself stripped to the waist.]* Dere! Dat's better! Now I kin breathe! *[Looking down at his feet, the spurs catch his eye]* And to hell wid dese high-fangled spurs. Dey're what's been a-trippin' me up an' breakin' me neck. *[He unstraps them and flings them away disgustedly.]* Dere! I gits rid o' dem frippety Emperor trappin's an' I travels lighter. Lawd! I'se tired! *[After a pause, listening to the insistent beat of the tom-tom in the distance]* I must 'a put some distance between myself an' dem – runnin' like dat – and yit – dat damn drum sound jes' de same – nearer, even. Well, I guess I a'most holds my lead anyhow. Dey won't never catch up. *[With a sigh]* If on'y my fool legs stands up. Oh, I'se sorry I evah went in for dis. Dat Emperor job is sho' hard to shake. *[He looks around him suspiciously.]* How'd dis road evah git heah? Good level road, too. I never remembers seein' it befo'. *[Shaking his head apprehensively]* Dese woods is sho' full o' de queerest things at night.

[*With a sudden terror*] Lawd God, don't let me see no more o' dem ha'nts! Dey gits me scared! [*Then trying to talk himself into confidence*] Ha'nts! You fool nigger, dey ain't no such things! Don't de Baptist parson tell you dat many time? Is you civilized, or is you like dese ign'rent black niggers heah? Sho'! Dat was all in yo' own head. Wasn't nothin' dere. Wasn't no Jeff! Know what? You jus' get seein' dem things 'cause yo' belly's empty and you's sick wid hunger inside. Hunger 'fects yo' head and yo' eyes. Any fool know dat. [*Then pleading fervently*] But bless God, I don't come across no more o' dem, whatever dey is! [*Then cautiously*] Rest! Don't talk! Rest! You needs it. Den you gits on yo' way again. [*Looking at the moon*] Night's half gone a'most. You hits de coast in de mawning! Den you'se all safe.

[*From the right forward a small gang of Negroes enter. They are dressed in striped convict suits, their heads are shaven, one leg drags limpingly, shackled to a heavy ball and chain. Some carry picks, the others shovels. They are followed by a white man dressed in the uniform of a* PRISON GUARD. *A Winchester rifle is slung across his shoulders and he carries a heavy whip. At a signal from the guard they stop on the road opposite where* JONES *is sitting.* JONES, *who has been staring up at the sky, unmindful of their noiseless approach, suddenly looks down and sees them. His eyes pop out, he tries to get to his feet and fly, but sinks back, too numbed by fright to move. His voice catches in a choking prayer*]

JONES : Lawd Jesus!

[*The* PRISON GUARD *cracks his whip – noiselessly – and at that signal all the* CONVICTS *start at work on the road. They swing their picks, they shovel, but not a sound comes from their labour. Their movements, like those of* JEFF *in the preceding scene, are those of automatons – rigid, slow, and mechanical. The* PRISON GUARD *points sternly at* JONES *with his whip, motions him to take his place among the other shovellers.* JONES *gets to his feet in a hypnotized stupor. He mumbles subserviently*]

JONES: Yes, suh! Yes, suh! I'se comin'.

[*As he shuffles, dragging one foot, over to his place, he curses under his breath with rage and hatred*]

JONES: God damn yo' soul, I gits even wid you yit, some time.

[*As if there were a shovel in his hands he goes through weary, mechanical gestures of digging up dirt, and throwing it to the roadside. Suddenly the* GUARD *approaches him angrily, threateningly. He raises his whip and lashes* JONES *viciously across the shoulders with it.* JONES *winces with pain and cowers abjectly. The* GUARD *turns his back on him and walks away contemptuously. Instantly* JONES *straightens up. With arms upraised as if his shovel were a club in his hands he springs murderously at the unsuspecting guard. In the act of crashing down his shovel on the white man's skull,* JONES *suddenly becomes aware that his hands are empty. He cries despairingly*]

JONES: Whar's my shovel? Gimme my shovel 'till I splits his damn head! [*Appealing to his fellow* CONVICTS] Gimme a shovel, one o' you, fo' God's sake!

[*They stand fixed in motionless attitudes, their eyes on the ground. The* GUARD *seems to wait expectantly, his back turned to the attacker.* JONES *bellows with baffled, terrified rage, tugging frantically at his revolver*]

JONES: I kills you, you white debil, if it's de last thing I evah does! Ghost or debil, I kill you agin!

[*He frees the revolver and fires point blank at the* GUARD'S *back. Instantly the walls of the forest close in from both sides, the road and the figures of the* CONVICT GANG *are blotted out in an enshrouding darkness. The only sounds are a crashing in the underbrush as* JONES *leaps away in mad flight and the throbbing of the tom-tom, still far distant, but increased in volume of sound and rapidity of beat.*]

SCENE FIVE

One o'clock. A large circular clearing, enclosed by the serried ranks of gigantic trunks of tall trees whose tops are lost to view. In the centre is a big dead stump worn by time into a curious resemblance to an auction block. The moon floods the clearing with a clear light.

[JONES *forces his way in through the forest on the left. He looks wildly about the clearing with hunted, fearful glances. His trousers are in tatters, his shoes cut and misshapen, flapping about his feet. He slinks cautiously to the stump in the centre and sits down in a tense position, ready for instant flight. Then he holds his head in his hands and rocks back and forth, moaning to himself miserably.*]

JONES: Oh Lawd, Lawd! Oh Lawd, Lawd! [*Suddenly he throws himself on his knees and raises his clasped hands to the sky – in a voice of agonized pleading.*] Lawd Jesus, heah my prayer! I'se a po' sinner, a po' sinner! I knows I done wrong, I knows it! When I cotches Jeff cheatin' wid loaded dice my anger overcomes me and I kills him dead! Lawd, I done wrong! When dat guard hits me wid de whip, my anger overcomes me, and I kills him dead. Lawd, I done wrong! And down heah whar dese fool bush niggers raises me up to the seat o' de mighty, I steals all I could grab. Lawd, I done wrong! I knows it! I'se sorry! Forgive me, Lawd! Forgive dis po' sinner! [*Then beseeching terrifiedly*] And keep dem away, Lawd! Keep dem away from me! And stop dat drum soundin' in my ears! Dat begin to sound ha'nted, too. [*He gets to his feet, evidently slightly reassured by his prayer – with attempted confidence.*] De Lawd'll preserve me from dem ha'nts after dis. [*Sits down on the stump again.*] I ain't skeered o' real men. Let dem come. But dem odders – [*He shudders – then looks down at his feet, working his toes inside the shoes –*

with a groan.] Oh, my po' feet! Dem shoes ain't no use no more 'ceptin' to hurt. I'se better off widout dem. [*He unlaces them and pulls them off – holds the wrecks of the shoes in his hands and regards them mournfully.*] You was real, A-one patin' leather, too. Look at you now. Emperor, you'se gittin' mighty low!

[*He sighs dejectedly and remains with bowed shoulders, staring down at the shoes in his hands as if reluctant to throw them away. While his attention is thus occupied, a crowd of figures silently enter the clearing from all sides. All are dressed in Southern costumes of the period of the fifties of the last century. There are middle-aged men who are evidently well-to-do* PLANTERS. *There is one spruce, authoritative individual – the* AUCTIONEER. *There are a crowd of curious spectators, chiefly young belles and dandies who have come to the slave-market for diversion. All exchange courtly greetings in dumb show and chat silently together. There is something stiff, rigid, unreal, marionettish about their movements. They group themselves about the stump. Finally a batch of slaves are led in from the left by an attendant – three men of different ages, two women, one with a baby in her arms, nursing. They are placed to the left of the stump, beside* JONES.

The WHITE PLANTERS *look them over appraisingly as if they were cattle. The dandies point their fingers and make witty remarks. The belles titter bewitchingly. All this in silence save for the ominous throb of the tom-tom. The* AUCTIONEER *holds up his hand, taking his place at the stump. The groups strain forward. He touches* JONES *on the shoulder peremptorily, motioning for him to stand on the stump – the auction block.*

JONES *looks up, sees the figures on all sides, looks wildly for some opening to escape, sees none, screams, and leaps madly to the top of the stump to get as far away from them as possible. He stands there, cowering, paralysed with horror. The* AUCTIONEER *begins his silent speech. He points to* JONES, *appeals to the planters to see for themselves. Here is a good field hand, sound in wind and limb as they can see. Very strong still in spite of his being middle-aged. Look at that back. Look at those shoulders. Look at the muscles in his arms and his sturdy legs. Capable of any amount of hard labour. Moreover of a good disposition, intelligent and tractable. Will any gentleman start the bidding? The planters raise their fingers, make their bids. They are apparently all eager to possess* JONES. *The bidding is lively, the crowd interested. While this has been going on,* JONES *has been seized by the courage of desperation. He dares to look down and around him. Over his face abject terror gives way to mystification, to gradual realization – stutteringly.*]

JONES: What you all doin', white folks? What's all dis? What you all lookin' at me fo'? What you doin' wid me, anyhow? [*Suddenly convulsed with raging hatred and fear*] Is dis a auction? Is you sellin' me like dey uster befo' de war? [*Jerking out his revolver just as the* AUCTIONEER *knocks him down to one of the planters – glaring from him to the purchaser*] And *you* sells me? And *you* buys me? I shows you I'se a free nigger, damn yo' souls!

[*He fires at the* AUCTIONEER *and at the* PLANTER *with such rapidity that the two shots are almost simultaneous. As if this were a signal the walls of the forest fold in. Only blackness remains and silence broken by* JONES *as he rushes off, crying with fear – and by the quickened, ever louder beat of the tom-tom.*]

SCENE SIX

Three o'clock. A cleared space in the forest. The limbs of the trees meet over it forming a low ceiling about five feet from the ground. The interlocked ropes of creepers reaching upward to entwine the tree trunks give an arched appearance to the sides. The space thus enclosed is like the dark, noisome hold of some ancient vessel. The moonlight is almost completely shut out and only a vague, wan light filters through.

[*There is the noise of someone approaching from the left, stumbling and crawling through the undergrowth.* JONES'S *voice is heard between chattering moans.*]

JONES: Oh, Lawd, what I gwine do now? Ain't got no bullet left on'y de silver one. If mo' o' dem ha'nts come after me, how I gwine skeer dem away? Oh, Lawd, on'y de silver one left – an' I gotta save dat fo' luck. If I shoots dat one I'm a goner sho'! Lawd, it's black heah! Whar's de moon? Oh, Lawd, don't dis night evah come to an end? [*By the sounds, he is feeling his way cautiously forward.*] Dere! Dis feels like a clear space. I gotta lie down an' rest. I don't care if dem niggers does cotch me. I gotta rest.

[*He is well forward now where his figure can be dimly made out. His trousers have been so torn away that what is left of them is no better than a loin-cloth. He flings himself full length, face downward on the ground, panting with exhaustion. Gradually it seems to grow lighter in the enclosed space and two rows of seated figures can be seen behind* JONES. *They are sitting in crumpled, despairing attitudes, hunched, facing one another with their backs touching the forest walls as if they were shackled to them. All are Negroes naked save for loin-cloths. At first they are silent and motionless. Then they begin to sway slowly forward toward each and back again in unison, as if they were laxly letting themselves follow the long roll of a ship at sea. At the same time a low, melancholy murmur rises among them, increasing gradually by rhythmic degrees which seem to be directed and controlled by the throb of the tom-tom in the distance, to a long, tremulous wail of despair that reaches a certain pitch, unbearably acute, then falls by slow gradations of tone into silence and is taken up again.* JONES *starts, looks up, sees the figures, and throws himself down again to shut out the sight. A shudder of terror shakes his whole body as the wail rises up about him again. But the next time his voice, as if under some uncanny compulsion, starts with the others. As their chorus lifts he rises to a sitting posture similar to the others, swaying back and forth. His voice reaches the highest pitch of sorrow, or desolation. The light fades out, the other voices cease, and only darkness is left.* JONES *can be heard scrambling to his feet and running off, his voice sinking down the scale and receding as he moves farther and farther away in the forest. The tom-tom beats louder, quicker, with a more insistent, triumphant pulsation.*]

SCENE SEVEN

Five o'clock. The foot of a gigantic tree by the edge of a great river. A rough structure of boulders, like an altar, is by the tree. The raised river bank is in the nearer background. Beyond this the surface of the river spreads out, brilliant and unruffled in the moonlight, blotted out and merged in a veil of bluish mist in the distance.

> [JONES'S *voice is heard from the left rising and falling in the long, despairing wail of the chained slaves, to the rhythmic beat of the tom-tom. As his voice sinks into silence, he enters the open space. The expression of his face is fixed and stony, his eyes have an obsessed glare, he moves with a strange deliberation like a sleep-walker or one in a trance. He looks around at the tree, the rough stone altar, the moonlit surface of the river beyond, and passes his hand over his head with a vague gesture of puzzled bewilderment. Then, as if in obedience to some obscure impulse, he sinks into a kneeling, devotional posture before the altar. Then he seems to come to himself partly, to have an uncertain realization of what he is doing, for he straightens up and stares about him horrifiedly – in an incoherent mumble*]

JONES: What – what is I doin'? What is – dis place? Seems like – seems like I know dat tree – an' dem stones – an' de river. I remember – seems like I been heah befo'. [*Tremblingly*] Oh, Gorry, I'se skeered in dis place! I'se skeered! Oh, Lawd, pertect dis sinner!

> [*Crawling away from the altar, he cowers close to the ground, his face hidden, his shoulders heaving with sobs of hysterical fright. From behind the trunk of the tree, as if he had sprung out of it, the figure of the Congo* WITCH-DOCTOR *appears. He is wizened and old, naked except for the fur of some small animal tied about his waist, its bushy tail hanging down in*

127

front. His body is stained all over a bright red. Antelope horns are on each side of his head, branching upward. In one hand he carries a bone rattle, in the other a charm stick with a bunch of white cockatoo feathers tied to the end. A great number of glass beads and bone ornaments are about his neck, ears, wrists, and ankles. He struts noiselessly with a queer prancing step to a position in the clear ground between JONES *and the altar. Then with a preliminary, summoning stamp of his foot on the earth, he begins to dance and to chant. As if in response to his summons the beating of the tom-tom grows to a fierce, exultant boom whose throbs seem to fill the air with vibrating rhythm.* JONES *looks up, starts to spring to his feet, reaches a half-kneeling, half-squatting position and remains rigidly fixed there, paralysed with awed fascination by this new apparition. The* WITCH-DOCTOR *sways, stamping with his foot, his bone rattle clicking the time. His voice rises and falls in a weird, monotonous croon, without articulate word divisions. Gradually his dance becomes clearly one of a narrative in pantomime, his croon is an incantation, a charm to allay the fierceness of some implacable deity demanding sacrifice. He flees, he is pursued by devils, he hides, he flees again. Ever wilder and wilder becomes his flight, nearer and nearer draws the pursuing evil, more and more the spirit of terror gains possession of him. His croon, rising to intensity, is punctuated by shrill cries.* JONES *has become completely hypnotized. His voice joins in the incantation, in the cries, he beats time with his hands and sways his body to and fro from the waist. The whole spirit and meaning of the dance has entered into him, has become his spirit. Finally the theme of the pantomime halts on a howl of despair, and is taken up again in a note of savage hope. There is a salvation. The forces of evil demand sacrifice. They must be appeased. The* WITCH-DOCTOR *points with his wand to the sacred tree, to the river beyond, to the altar, and finally to* JONES *with a ferocious command.* JONES *seems to sense the meaning of this. It is he who must offer himself for sacrifice.*

He beats his forehead abjectly to the ground, moaning hysterically.]

JONES: Mercy, oh Lawd! Mercy! Mercy on dis po' sinner.

[*The* WITCH-DOCTOR *springs to the river bank. He stretches out his arms and calls to some god within its depths. Then he starts backward slowly, his arms remaining out. A huge head of a crocodile appears over the bank and its eyes, glittering greenly, fasten upon* JONES. *He stares into them fascinatedly. The* WITCH-DOCTOR *prances up to him, touches him with his wand, motions with hideous command towards the waiting monster.* JONES *squirms on his belly nearer and nearer, moaning continually.*]

JONES: Mercy, Lawd! Mercy!

[*The crocodile heaves more of his enormous hulk on to the land.* JONES *squirms toward him. The* WITCH-DOCTOR'S *voice shrills out in furious exultation, the tom-tom beats madly.* JONES *cries out in a fierce, exhausted spasm of anguished pleading.*]

JONES: Lawd, save me! Lawd Jesus, heah my prayer!

[*Immediately, in answer to his prayer, comes the thought of the one bullet left him. He snatches at his hip, shouting defiantly.*]

JONES: De silver bullet! You don't git me yit!

[*He fires at the green eyes in front of him. The head of the crocodile sinks back behind the river bank, the* WITCH-DOCTOR *springs behind the sacred tree and disappears.* JONES *lies with his face to the ground, his arms outstretched, whimpering with fear as the throb of the tom-tom fills the silence about him with a sombre pulsation, a baffled but revengeful power.*]

SCENE EIGHT

Dawn. Same as Scene Two, the dividing line of forest and plain. The nearest tree trunks are dimly revealed, but the forest behind them is still a mass of glooming shadow. The tom-tom seems on the very spot, so loud and continuously vibrating are its beats.

> [LEM *enters from the left, followed by a small squad of his* SOLDIERS, *and by the Cockney trader,* SMITHERS. LEM *is a heavy-set, ape-faced old savage of the extreme African type, dressed only in a loin-cloth. A revolver and cartridge belt are about his waist. His* SOLDIERS *are in different degrees of rag-concealed nakedness. All wear broad palm-leaf hats. Each one carries a rifle.* SMITHERS *is the same as in Scene One. One of the soldiers, evidently a tracker, is peering about keenly on the ground. He grunts and points to the spot where* JONES *entered the forest.* LEM *and* SMITHERS *come to look.*]

SMITHERS [*after a glance, turns away in disgust*]: That's where 'e went in right enough. Much good it'll do yer. 'E's miles orf by this an' safe to the coast, damn 's 'ide! I tole yer yer'd lose 'im, didn't I? – wastin' the 'ole bloomin' night beatin' yer bloody drum and castin' yer silly spells! Gawd blimey, wot a pack!

LEM [*gutturally*]: We cotch him. You see. [*He makes a motion to his soldiers who squat down on their haunches in a semi-circle.*]

SMITHERS [*exasperatedly*]: Well, ain't yer goin' in an' 'unt 'im in the woods? What the 'ell's the good of waitin'?

LEM [*imperturbably – squatting down himself*]: We cotch him.

SMITHERS [*turning away from him contemptuously*]: Aw! Garn! 'E's a better man than the lot o' you put together. I 'ates the sight o' 'im, but I'll say that for 'im.

> [*A sound of snapping twigs comes from the forest. The* SOLDIERS *jump to their feet, cocking their rifles alertly.*

LEM *remains sitting with an imperturbable expression, but listening intently. The sound from the woods is repeated.* LEM *makes a quick signal with his hand. His followers creep quickly but noiselessly into the forest, scattering so that each enters at a different spot.*]

SMITHERS [*in the silence that follows – in a contemptuous whisper*]: You ain't thinkin' that would be 'im, I 'ope?

LEM [*calmly*]: We cotch him.

SMITHERS: Blarsted fat 'eads! [*Then after a second's thought – wonderingly*] Still, after all, it might 'appen. If 'e lost 'is bloody way in these stinkin' woods 'e'd likely turn in a circle without 'is knowin' it. They all does.

LEM [*peremptorily*]: Ssshh! [*The reports of several rifles sound from the forest, followed a second later by savage, exultant yells. The beating of the tom-tom abruptly ceases.* LEM *looks up at the white man with a grin of satisfaction.*] We cotch him. Him dead.

SMITHERS [*with a snarl*]: 'Ow d'yer know it's 'im, an' 'ow d'yer know 'e's dead?

LEM: My mens dey got 'um silver bullets. Dey kill him shure.

SMITHERS [*astonished*]: They got silver bullets?

LEM: Lead bullet no kill him. He got um strong charm. I cook um money, make um silver bullet, make um strong charm, too.

SMITHERS [*light breaking upon him*]: So that's wot you was up to all night, wot? You was scared to put after 'im till you'd moulded silver bullets, eh?

LEM [*simply stating a fact*]: Yes. Him got strong charm. Lead no good.

SMITHERS [*slapping his thigh and guffawing*]: Haw-haw! If yer don't beat all 'ell! [*Then recovering himself – scornfully*] I'll bet yer it ain't 'im they shot at all, yer bleedin' looney!

LEM [*calmly*]: Dey come bring him now. [*The* SOLDIERS *come out of the forest, carrying* JONES'S *limp body. There is a little reddish-purple hole under his left breast. He is dead. They carry him to* LEM, *who examines his body with great satisfaction.*]

SMITHERS [*leans over his shoulder – in a tone of frightened awe*]: Well, they did for yer right enough, Jonesy, me lad! Dead as a bloater! [*Mockingly*] Where's yer 'igh an' mighty airs now, yer bloomin' Majesty? [*Then with a grin*] Silver bullets! Gawd blimey, but yer died in the 'eighth o' style, any'ow! [LEM *makes a motion to the soldiers to carry the body out, left.* SMITHERS *speaks to him sneeringly.*] And I s'pose you think it's yer bleedin' charms and yer silly beatin' the drum that made 'im run in a circle when 'e'd lost 'imself, don't yer? [*But* LEM *makes no reply, does not seem to hear the question, walks out, left, after his men.* SMITHERS *looks after him with contemptuous scorn.*] Stupid as 'ogs, the lot of 'em! Blarsted niggers!

THE CURTAIN FALLS

DESIRE UNDER THE ELMS

A Play in Three Parts

CHARACTERS

Ephraim Cabot

Simeon }
Peter   } His sons
Eben   }

Abbie Putnam

Young Girl; Two Farmers; the Fiddler; a Sheriff; and other people from the surrounding farms.

DESIRE UNDER THE ELMS

THE action of the entire play takes place in, and immediately outside of, the Cabot farm-house in New England, in the year 1850. The south end of the house faces a stone wall with a wooden gate at centre opening on a country road. The house is in good condition, but in need of paint. Its walls are a sickly greyish, the green of the shutters faded. Two enormous elms are on each side of the house. They bend their trailing branches down over the roof – they appear to protect and at the same time subdue; there is a sinister maternity in their aspect, a crushing, jealous absorption. When the wind does not keep them astir, they develop from their intimate contact with the life of man in the house an appalling humanness. They brood oppressively over the house, they are like exhausted women resting their sagging breasts and hands and hair on its roof, and when it rains their tears trickle down monotonously and rot on the shingles.

There is a path running from the gate around the right corner of the house to the front door. A narrow porch is on this side. The end wall facing us has two windows in its upper story, two larger ones on the floor below. The two upper are those of the father's bedroom and that of the brothers. On the left, ground floor, is the kitchen – on the right, the parlour, the blinds of which are always pulled down.

PART ONE

SCENE 1

Exterior of the farm-house. It is sunset of a day at the beginning of summer in the year 1850. There is no wind and everything is still. The sky above the roof is suffused with deep colours, the green of the elms glows, but the house is in shadow, seeming pale and washed out by contrast.

[*A door opens and* EBEN CABOT *comes to the end of the porch and stands looking down the road to the right. He has a large bell in his hand and this he swings mechanically, awakening a deafening clangour. Then he puts his hands on his hips and stares up at the sky. He sighs with a puzzled awe and blurts out with halting appreciation.*]

EBEN: God! Purty!

[*His eyes fall and he stares about him frowningly. He is twenty-five, tall, and sinewy. His face is well formed, good-looking, but its expression is resentful and defensive. His defiant dark eyes remind one of a wild animal's in captivity. Each day is a cage in which he finds himself trapped, but inwardly unsubdued. There is a fierce repressed vitality about him. He has black hair, moustache, a thin curly trace of beard. He is dressed in rough farm clothes.*

He spits on the ground with intense disgust, turns and goes back into the house.

SIMEON *and* PETER *come in from their work in the fields. They are tall men, much older than their half-brother (*SIMEON *is thirty-nine and* PETER *thirty-seven), built on a squarer, simpler model, fleshier in body, more bovine and homelier in face, shrewder, and more practical. Their shoulders stoop a bit*

137

*from years of farm work. They clump heavily along in their
clumsy thick-soled boots caked with earth. Their clothes, their
faces, hands, bare arms and throats are earth-stained. They smell
of earth. They stand together for a moment in front of the house
and, as if with the one impulse, stare dumbly up at the sky,
leaning on their hoes. Their faces have a compressed, un-
resigned expression. As they look upward, this softens.*]

SIMEON [*grudgingly*]: Purty.

PETER: Ay-eh.

SIMEON [*suddenly*]: Eighteen year ago.

PETER: What?

SIMEON: Jenn. My woman. She died.

PETER: I'd fergot.

SIMEON: I rec'lect – now an' agin. Makes it lonesome. She'd
hair long's a hoss's tail – an' yaller like gold!

PETER: Waal – she's gone. [*This with indifferent finality – then
after a pause*] They's gold in the West, Sim.

SIMEON [*still under the influence of sunset – vaguely*]: In the sky?

PETER: Waal – in a manner o' speakin' – thar's the promise.
[*Growing excited*] Gold in the sky – in the west – Golden
Gate – Californi-a! – Golden West! – fields o' gold!

SIMEON [*excited in his turn*]: Fortunes layin' just atop o' the
ground waitin' t' be picked! Solomon's mines, they says!
[*For a moment they continue looking up at the sky – then their
eyes drop.*]

PETER [*with sardonic bitterness*]: Here – it's stones atop o' the
ground – stones atop o' stones – makin' stone walls – year
atop o' year – him 'n' yew 'n' me 'n' then Eben – makin'
stone walls fur him to fence us in!

SIMEON: We've wuked. Give our strength. Give our years.
Ploughed 'em under in the ground [*he stamps rebelliously*] –
rottin' – makin' soil for his crops! [*A pause*] Waal – the
farm pays good for hereabouts.

PETER: If we ploughed in Californi-a, they'd be lumps o'
gold in the furrow –!

SIMEON: Californi-a's t'other side o' earth, a'most. We got t' calc'late –

PETER [*after a pause*]: 'Twould be hard fur me, too, to give up what we've 'arned here by our sweat. [*A pause.* EBEN *sticks his head out of the dining-room window, listening.*]

SIMEON: Ay-eh. [*A pause*] Mebbe – he'll die soon.

PETER [*doubtfully*]: Mebbe.

SIMEON: Mebbe – fur all we knows – he's dead now.

PETER: Ye'd need proof –

SIMEON: He's been gone two months – with no word.

PETER: Left us in the fields an evenin' like this. Hitched up an' druv off into the West. That's plumb onnateral. He hain't never been off this farm 'ceptin' t' the village in thirty year or more, not since he married Eben's maw. [*A pause. Shrewdly*] I calc'late we might git him declared crazy by the court.

SIMEON: He skinned 'em too slick. He got the best o' all on 'em. They'd never b'lieve him crazy. [*A pause*] We got t' wait – till he's under ground.

EBEN [*with a sardonic chuckle*]: Honour thy father! [*They turn, startled, and stare at him. He grins, then scowls.*] I pray he's died. [*They stare at him. He continues matter-of-factly.*] Supper's ready.

SIMEON *and* PETER [*together*]: Ay-eh.

EBEN [*gazing up at the sky*]: Sun's downin' purty.

SIMEON *and* PETER [*together*]: Ay-eh. They's gold in the West.

EBEN: Ay-eh. [*Pointing*] Yonder atop o' the hill pasture, ye mean?

SIMEON *and* PETER [*together*]: In Californi-a!

EBEN: Hunh? [*Stares at them indifferently for a second, then drawls.*] Waal – supper's gittin' cold. [*He turns back into kitchen.*]

SIMEON [*startled – smacks his lips*]: I air hungry!

PETER [*sniffing*]: I smells bacon!

SIMEON [*with hungry appreciation*]: Bacon's good!

PETER [*in same tone*]: Bacon's bacon!

[*They turn, shouldering each other, their bodies bumping and rubbing together as they hurry clumsily to their food, like two friendly oxen toward their evening meal. They disappear around the right corner of house and can be heard entering the door.*]

CURTAIN

SCENE 2

The colour fades from the sky. Twilight begins. The interior of the kitchen is now visible. A pine table is at centre, a cooking-stove in the right rear corner, four rough wooden chairs, a tallow candle on the table. In the middle of the rear wall is fastened a big advertising poster with a ship in full sail and the word 'California' in big letters. Kitchen utensils hang from nails. Everything is neat and in order, but the atmosphere is of a men's camp kitchen rather than that of a home.

[*Places for three are laid.* EBEN *takes boiled potatoes and bacon from the stove and puts them on the table, also a loaf of bread and a crock of water.* SIMEON *and* PETER *shoulder in, slump down in their chairs without a word.* EBEN *joins them. The three eat in silence for a moment, the two elder as naturally unrestrained as beasts of the field,* EBEN *picking at his food without appetite, glancing at them with a tolerant dislike.*]

SIMEON [*suddenly turns to* EBEN]: Looky here! Ye'd oughtn't t' said that, Eben.

PETER: 'Twa'n't righteous.

EBEN: What?

SIMEON: Ye prayed he'd die.

EBEN: Waal – don't yew pray it? [*A pause*]

PETER: He's our Paw.

EBEN [*violently*]: Not mine!

SIMEON [*dryly*]: Ye'd not let no one else say that about yer Maw! Ha! [*He gives one abrupt sardonic guffaw.* PETER *grins.*]

EBEN [*very pale*]: I meant – I hain't his'n – I hain't like him – he hain't me –

PETER [*dryly*]: Wait till ye've growed his age!

EBEN [*intensely*]: I'm Maw – every drop o' blood! [*A pause. They stare at him with indifferent curiosity.*]

PETER [*reminiscently*]: She was good t' Sim 'n' me. A good step-maw's scurse.

SIMEON: She was good t' every one.

EBEN [*greatly moved, gets to his feet and makes an awkward bow to each of them – stammering*]: I be thankful t' ye. I'm her. Her heir. [*He sits down in confusion.*]

PETER [*after a pause – judicially*]: She was good even t' him.

EBEN [*fiercely*]: An' fur thanks he killed her!

SIMEON [*after a pause*]: No one never kills nobody. It's allus somethin'. That's the murderer.

EBEN: Didn't he slave Maw t' death?

PETER: He's slaved himself t' death. He's slaved Sim 'n' me 'n' yew t' death – on'y none o' us hain't died – yit.

SIMEON: It's somethin' – drivin' him – t' drive us –

EBEN [*vengefully*]: Waal – I hold him t' jedgement! [*Then scornfully*] Somethin'! What's somethin'?

SIMEON: Dunno.

EBEN [*sardonically*]: What's drivin' yew to Californi-a, mebbe? [*They look at him in surprise.*] Oh, I've heerd ye! [*Then, after a pause*] But ye'll never go t' the gold-fields!

PETER [*assertively*]: Mebbe!

EBEN: Whar'll ye git the money?

PETER: We kin walk. It's an a'mighty ways – Californi-a – but if yew was t' put all the steps we've walked on this farm end t' end we'd be in the moon!

EBEN: The Injuns'll skulp ye on the plains.

SIMEON [*with grim humour*]: We'll mebbe make 'em pay a hair fur a hair!

EBEN [*decisively*]: But 'tain't that. Ye won't never go because ye'll wait here fur yer share o' the farm, thinkin' allus he'll die soon.

SIMEON [*after a pause*]: We've a right.

PETER: Two-thirds belongs t' us.

EBEN [*jumping to his feet*]: Ye've no right! She wa'n't yewr Maw! It was her farm! Didn't he steal it from her? She's dead. It's my farm.

SIMEON [*sardonically*]: Tell that t' Paw – when he comes! I'll bet ye a dollar he'll laugh – fur once in his life. Ha! [*He laughs himself in one single mirthless bark.*]

PETER [*amused in turn, echoes his brother*]: Ha!

SIMEON [*after a pause*]: What've ye got held agin us, Eben? Year arter year it's skulked in yer eye – somethin'.

PETER: Ay-eh.

EBEN: Ay-eh. They's somethin'. [*Suddenly exploding*] Why didn't ye never stand between him 'n' my Maw when he was slavin' her to her grave – t' pay her back fur the kindness she done t' yew? [*There is a long pause. They stare at him in surprise.*]

SIMEON: Waal – the stock'd got t' be watered.

PETER: 'R they was woodin' t' do.

SIMEON: 'R ploughin'.

PETER: 'R hayin'.

SIMEON: 'R spreadin' manure.

PETER: 'R weedin'.

SIMEON: 'R prunin'.

PETER: 'R milkin'.

EBEN [*breaking in harshly*]: An' makin' walls – stone atop stone – makin' walls till yer heart's a stone ye heft up out the way o' growth on to a stone wall t' wall in yer heart!

SIMEON [*matter-of-factly*]: We never had no time t' meddle.

PETER [*to* EBEN]: Yew was fifteen afore yer Maw died – an'
big fur yer age. Why didn't ye never do nothin'?

EBEN [*harshly*]: They was chores t' do, wa'n't they? [*A pause –
then slowly*] It was on'y arter she died I come to think o' it.
Me cookin' – doin' her work – that made me know her,
suffer her sufferin' – she'd come back t' help – come back
t' bile potatoes – come back t' fry bacon – come back t'
bake biscuits – come back all cramped up t' shake the fire,
an' carry ashes, her eyes weepin' an' bloody with smoke an'
cinders same's they used t' be. She still comes back – stands
by the stove thar in the evenin' – she can't find it nateral
sleepin' an' restin' in peace. She can't git used t' bein' free –
even in her grave.

SIMEON: She never complained none.

EBEN: She'd got too tired. She'd got too used t' bein' too
tired. That was what he done. [*With vengeful passion*] An'
sooner'r later, I'll meddle. I'll say the thin's I didn't say then
t' him! I'll yell 'em at the top o' my lungs. I'll see t' it my
Maw gits some rest an' sleep in her grave! [*He sits down again,
relapsing into a brooding silence. They look at him with a queer
indifferent curiosity.*]

PETER [*after a pause*]: Whar in tarnation d'ye s'pose he went,
Sim?

SIMEON: Dunno. He druv off in the buggy, all spick an' span,
with the mare all breshed an' shiny, druv off clackin' his
tongue an' wavin' his whip. I remember it right well. I
was finishin' ploughin', it was spring an' May an' sunset, an'
gold in the West, an' he druv off into it. I yells 'Whar ye
goin', Paw?' an' he hauls up by the stone wall a jiffy. His
old snake's eyes was glitterin' in the sun like he'd been
drinkin' a jugful an' he says with a mule's grin: 'Don't ye
run away till I come back!'

PETER: Wonder if he knowed we was wantin' fur Californi-a?

SIMEON: Mebbe. I didn't say nothin' and he says, lookin' kin-
der queer an' sick: 'I been hearin' the hens cluckin' an' the

roosters crowin' all the durn day. I been listenin' t' the cows lowin' an' everythin' else kickin' up till I can't stand it no more. It's spring an' I'm feelin' damned,' he says. 'Damned like an old bare hickory tree fit on'y fur burnin','he says. An' then I calc'late I must've looked a mite hopeful, fur he adds real spry and vicious: 'But don't git no fool idee I'm dead. I've sworn t' live a hundred an' I'll do it, if on'y t' spite yer sinful greed! An' now I'm ridin' out t' learn God's message t' me in the spring, like the prophets done. An' yew git back t' yer ploughin',' he says. An' he druv off singin' a hymn. I thought he was drunk – 'r I'd stopped him goin'.

EBEN [*scornfully*]: No, ye wouldn't! Ye're scared o' him. He's stronger – inside – than both o' ye put together!

PETER [*sardonically*]: An' yew – be yew Samson?

EBEN: I'm gittin' stronger. I kin feel it growin' in me – growin' an' growin' – till it'll bust out –! [*He gets up and puts on his coat and a hat. They watch him, gradually breaking into grins.* EBEN *avoids their eyes sheepishly.*] I'm goin' out fur a spell – up the road.

PETER: T' the village?

SIMEON: T' see Minnie?

EBEN [*defiantly*]: Ay-eh!

PETER [*jeeringly*]: The Scarlet Woman!

SIMEON: Lust – that's what's growin' in ye!

EBEN: Waal – she' s purty!

PETER: She's been purty fur twenty year!

SIMEON: A new coat o' paint'll make a heifer out of forty.

EBEN: She hain't forty!

PETER: If she hain't, she's teeterin' on the edge.

EBEN [*desperately*]: What d'yew know –?

PETER: All they is . . . Sim knew her – an' then me arter –

SIMEON: An' Paw kin tell yew somethin', too! He was fust!

EBEN: D'ye mean t' say he –?

SIMEON [*with a grin*]: Ay-eh! We air his heirs in everythin'!

EBEN [*intensely*]: That's more to it! That grows on it! It'll bust soon! [*Then violently*] I'll go smash my fist in her face! [*He pulls open the door in rear violently.*]

SIMEON [*with a wink at* PETER – *drawlingly*]: Mebbe – but the night's wa'm – purty – by the time ye git thar mebbe ye'll kiss her instead!

PETER: Sart'n he will!

[*They both roar with coarse laughter.* EBEN *rushes out and slams the door – then the outside front door – comes around the corner of the house and stands still by the gate, staring up at the sky.*]

SIMEON [*looking after him*]: Like his Paw!

PETER: Dead spit an' image!

SIMEON: Dog'll eat dog!

PETER: Ay-eh. [*Pause. With yearning*] Mebbe a year from now we'll be in Californi-a.

SIMEON: Ay-eh. [*A pause. Both yawn.*] Let's git t' bed.

[*He blows out the candle. They go out door in rear.* EBEN *stretches his arms up to the sky – rebelliously.*]

EBEN: Waal – thar's a star, an' somewhar's they's him, an' here's me, an' thar's Min up the road – in the same night. What if I does kiss her? She's like t'night, she's soft 'n' wa'm, her eyes kin wink like a star, her mouth's wa'm, her arms're wa'm, she smells like a wa'm ploughed field, she's purty. . . . Ay-eh! By God A'mighty she's purty, an' I don't give a damn how many sins she's sinned afore mine or who she's sinned 'em with, my sin's as purty as any one on 'em! [*He strides off down the road to the left.*]

SCENE 3

It is the pitch darkness just before dawn.

> [EBEN *comes in from the left and goes around to the porch, feeling his way, chuckling bitterly and cursing half-aloud to himself.*]

EBEN: The cussed old miser! [*He can be heard going in the front door. There is a pause as he goes upstairs, then a loud knock on the bedroom door of the brothers.*] Wake up!

SIMEON [*startled*]: Who's thar?

EBEN [*pushing open the door and coming in, a lighted candle in his hand. The bedroom of the brothers is revealed. Its ceiling is the sloping roof. They can stand upright only close to the centre dividing wall of the upstairs.* SIMEON *and* PETER *are in a double bed, front.* EBEN'S *cot is to the rear.* EBEN *has a mixture of silly grin and vicious scowl on his face*]: I be!

PETER [*angrily*]: What in hell fire —?

EBEN: I got news fur ye! Ha! [*He gives one abrupt sardonic guffaw.*]

SIMEON [*angrily*]: Couldn't ye hold it 'till we'd got our sleep?

EBEN: It's nigh sun up. [*Then explosively*] He's gone an' married agen!

SIMEON *and* PETER [*explosively*]: Paw?

EBEN: Got himself hitched to a female 'bout thirty-five – an' purty, they says –

SIMEON [*aghast*]: It's a durn lie!

PETER: Who says?

SIMEON: They been stringin' ye!

EBEN: Think I'm a dunce, do ye? The hull village says. The preacher from New Dover, he brung the news – told it t' our preacher – New Dover, that's whar the old loon got himself hitched – that's whar the woman lived –

PETER [*no longer doubting – stunned*]: Waal . . . !

SIMEON [*the same*]: Waal . . . !

EBEN [*sitting down on a bed – with vicious hatred*]: Ain't he a devil out o' hell? It's jest t' spite us – the damned old mule!

PETER [*after a pause*]: Everythin'll go t' her now.

SIMEON: Ay-eh. [*A pause – dully*] Waal – if it's done –

PETER: It's done us. [*Pause – then persuasively*] They's gold in the fields o' Californi-a, Sim. No good a-stayin' here now.

SIMEON: Jes what I was a-thinkin'. [*Then with decision*] 'S well fust's last! Let's lightout and git this mornin'.

PETER: Suits me.

EBEN: Ye must like walkin'.

SIMEON [*sardonically*]: If ye'd grow wings on us we'd fly thar!

EBEN: Ye'd like ridin' better – on a boat, wouldn't ye? [*Fumbles in his pocket and takes out a crumpled sheet of foolscap.*] Waal, if ye sign this ye kin ride on a boat. I've had it writ out an' ready in case ye'd ever go. It says fur three hundred dollars t' each ye agree yewr shares o' the farm is sold t' me. [*They look suspiciously at the paper. A pause.*]

SIMEON [*wonderingly*]: But if he's hitched agen –

PETER: An' whar'd yew git that sum o' money, anyways?

EBEN [*cunningly*]: I know whar it's hid. I been waitin' – Maw told me. She knew whar it lay fur years, but she was waitin'. . . . It's her'n – the money he hoarded from her farm an' hid from Maw. It's my money by rights now.

PETER: Whar's it hid?

EBEN [*cunningly*]: Whar yew won't never find it without me. Maw spied on him – 'r she'd never knowed. [*A pause. They look at him suspiciously, and he at them.*] Waal, is it fa'r trade?

SIMEON: Dunno.

PETER: Dunno.

SIMEON [*looking at window*]: Sky's greyin'.

PETER: Ye better start the fire, Eben.

SIMEON: An' fix some vittles.

EBEN: Ay-eh. [*Then with a forced jocular heartiness*] I'll git ye a good one. If ye're startin' t' hoof it t' California ye'll need somethin' that'll stick t' yer ribs. [*He turns to the door, adding meaningly*] But ye kin ride on a boat if ye'll swap. [*He stops at the door and pauses. They stare at him.*]

SIMEON [*suspiciously*]: Whar was ye all night?

EBEN [*defiantly*]: Up t' Min's. [*Then slowly*] Walkin' thar, fust I felt 's if I'd kiss her; then I got a-thinkin' o' what ye'd said o' him an' her an' I says, I'll bust her nose fur that! Then I got t' the village an' heerd the news an' I got mad- der'n hell an' run all the way t' Min's not knowin' what I'd do – [*He pauses – then sheepishly but more defiantly*] Waal – when I seen her, I didn't hit her – nor I didn't kiss her nuther – I begun t' beller like a calf an' cuss at the same time, I was so durn mad – an' she got scared – an' I jest grabbed holt an' tuk her! [*Proudly*] Yes, sirree! I tuk her. She may've been his'n – an' your'n, too – but she's mine now!

SIMEON [*dryly*]: In love, air yew?

EBEN [*with lofty scorn*]: Love! I don't take no stock in sech slop!

PETER [*winking at* SIMEON]: Mebbe Eben's aimin' t' marry, too.

SIMEON: Min'd make a true faithful he'pmeet – fur the army! [*They snicker.*]

EBEN: What do I care fur her – 'ceptin' she's round an' wa'm? The p'int is she was his'n – an' now she b'longs t' me! [*He goes to the door – then turns – rebelliously.*] An' Min hain't sech a bad un. They's worse'n Min in the world, I'll bet ye! Wait'll we see this cow the Old Man's hitched t'! She'll beat Min, I got a notion! [*He starts to go out.*]

SIMEON [*suddenly*]: Mebbe ye'll try t' make her your'n, too?

PETER: Ha! [*He gives a sardonic laugh of relish at this idea.*]

EBEN [*spitting with disgust*]: Her – here – sleepin' with him – stealin' my Maw's farm! I'd as soon pet a skunk 'r kiss a snake! [*He goes out. The two stare after him suspiciously. A pause. They listen to his steps receding.*]

PETER: He's startin' the fire.

SIMEON: I'd like t' ride t' Californi-a – but –

PETER: Min might 'a' put some scheme in his head.

SIMEON: Mebbe it's all a lie 'bout Paw marryin'. We'd best wait an' see the bride.

PETER: An' don't sign nothin' till we does –

SIMEON: Nor till we've tested it's good money! [*Then with a grin*] But if Paw's hitched we'd be sellin' Eben somethin' we'd never git nohow!

PETER: We'll wait an' see. [*Then with sudden vindictive anger*] An' till he comes, let's yew 'n' me not wuk a lick, let Eben tend to thin's if he's a mind t', let's us jest sleep an' eat an' drink likker, an' let the hull damned farm go t' blazes!

SIMEON [*excitedly*]: By God, we've 'arned a rest! We'll play rich fur a change. I hain't agoin' to stir outa bed till breakfast's ready.

PETER: An' on the table!

SIMEON [*after a pause – thoughtfully*]: What d'ye calc'late she'll be like – our new Maw? Like Eben thinks?

PETER: More'n likely.

SIMEON [*vindictively*]: Waal – I hope she's a she-devil that'll make him wish he was dead an' livin' in the pit o' hell fur comfort!

PETER [*fervently*]: Amen!

SIMEON [*imitating his father's voice*]: 'I'm ridin' out t' learn God's message t' me in the spring like the prophets done,' he says. I'll bet right then an' thar he knew plumb well he was goin' whorin', the stinkin' old hypocrite!

SCENE 4

Same as Scene 2 – shows the interior of the kitchen, with a lighted candle on table. It is grey dawn outside.

> [SIMEON *and* PETER *are just finishing their breakfast.* EBEN *sits before his plate of untouched food, brooding frowningly.*]

PETER [*glancing at him rather irritably*]: Lookin' glum don't help none.

SIMEON [*sarcastically*]: Sorrowin' over his lust o' the flesh.

PETER [*with a grin*]: Was she yer fust?

EBEN [*angrily*]: None o' yer business. [*A pause*] I was thinkin' o' him. I got a notion he's gittin' near – I kin feel him comin' on like yew kin feel malaria chill afore it takes ye.

PETER: It's too early yet.

SIMEON: Dunno. He'd like t' catch us nappin' – jest t' have somethin' t' hoss us 'round over.

PETER [*mechanically gets to his feet.* SIMEON *does the same*]: Waal – let's git t' wuk. [*They both plod mechanically toward the door before they realize. Then they stop short.*]

SIMEON [*grinning*]: Ye're a cussed fool, Pete – and I be wuss! Let him see we hain't wukin'! We don't give a durn!

PETER [*as they go back to the table*]: Not a damned durn! It'll serve t' show him we're done with him. [*They sit down again.* EBEN *stares from one to the other with surprise.*]

SIMEON [*grins at him*]: We're aimin' t' start bein' lilies o' the field.

PETER: Nary a toil 'r spin 'r lick o' wuk do we put in!

SIMEON: Ye're sole owner – till he comes – that's what ye wanted. Waal, ye got t' be sole hand, too.

PETER: The cows air bellerin'. Ye better hustle at the milkin'.

EBEN [*with excited joy*]: Ye mean ye'll sign the paper?

SIMEON [*dryly*]: Mebbe.

PETER: Mebbe.

SIMEON: We're considerin'. [*Peremptorily*] Ye better git t' wuk.

EBEN [*with queer excitement*]: It's Maw's farm agen! It's my farm! Them's my cows! I'll milk my durn fingers off fur cows o' mine! [*He goes out door in rear, they stare after him indifferently.*]

SIMEON: Like his Paw.

PETER: Dead spit 'n' image!

SIMEON: Waal – let dog eat dog!

[EBEN *comes out of front door and around the corner of the house. The sky is beginning to grow flushed with sunrise.* EBEN *stops by the gate and stares around him with glowing, possessive eyes. He takes in the whole farm with his embracing glance of desire.*]

EBEN: It's purty! It's damned purty! It's mine! [*He suddenly throws his head back boldly and glares with hard, defiant eyes at the sky.*] Mine, d'ye hear? Mine! [*He turns and walks quickly off left, rear, toward the barn. The two brothers light their pipes.*]

SIMEON [*putting his muddy boots up on the table, tilting back his chair, and puffing defiantly*]: Waal – this air solid comfort – fur once.

PETER: Ay-eh. [*He follows suit. A pause. Unconsciously they both sigh.*]

SIMEON [*suddenly*]: He never was much o' a hand at milkin', Eben wa'n't.

PETER [*with a snort*]: His hands air like hoofs! [*A pause*]

SIMEON: Reach down the jug thar! Let's take a swaller. I'm feelin' kind o' low.

PETER: Good idee! [*He does so – gets two glasses – they pour out drinks of whisky.*] Here's t' gold in Californi-a!

SIMEON: An' luck t' find it! [*They drink – puff resolutely – sigh – take their feet down from the table.*]

PETER: Likker don't 'pear t' sot right.

SIMEON: We hain't used t' it this early. [*A pause. They become very restless.*]

PETER: Gittin' close in this kitchen.

SIMEON [*with immense relief*]: Let's git a breath o' air.
[*They arise briskly and go out rear – appear around house and stop by the gate. They stare up at the sky with a numbed appreciation.*]

PETER: Purty!

SIMEON: Ay-eh. Gold's t' the East now.

PETER: Sun's startin' with us fur the Golden West.

SIMEON [*staring around the farm, his compressed lips tightened, unable to conceal his emotion*]: Waal – it's our last mornin' – mebbe.

PETER [*the same*]: Ay-eh.

SIMEON [*stamps his foot on the earth and addresses it desperately*]: Waal – ye've thirty year o' me buried in ye – spread out over ye – blood an' bone an' sweat – rotted away – fertilizin' ye – richin' yer soul – prime manure, by God, that's what I been t' ye!

PETER: Ay-eh! An' me!

SIMEON: An' yew, Peter. [*He sighs – then spits.*] Waal – no use'n cryin' over spilt milk.

PETER: They's gold in the West – an' freedom mebbe. We been slaves t' stone walls here.

SIMEON [*defiantly*]: We hain't nobody's slaves from this out – nor no thin's slaves nuther. [*A pause – restlessly*] Speakin' o' milk, wonder how Eben's managin'?

PETER: I s'pose he's managin'.

SIMEON: Mebbe we'd ought t' help – this once.

PETER: Mebbe. The cows knows us.

SIMEON: An' likes us. They don't know him much.

PETER: An' the hosses, an' pigs, an' chickens. They don't know him much.

SIMEON: They knows us like brothers – an' likes us! [*Proudly*] Hain't we raised 'em t' be fust-rate, number one prize stock?

PETER: We hain't – not no more.

SIMEON [*dully*]: I was fergittin'. [*Then resignedly*] Waal, let's go help Eben a spell an' git waked up.

PETER: Suits me.

[*They are starting off down left, rear, for the barn when* EBEN *appears from there hurrying toward them, his face excited.*]

EBEN [*breathlessly*]: Waal – har they be! The old mule an' the bride! I seen 'em from the barn down below at the turnin'.

PETER: How could ye tell that far?

EBEN: Hain't I as far-sight as he's near-sight? Don't I know the mare 'n' buggy, an' two people settin' in it? Who else . . .? An' I tell ye I kin feel 'em a-comin', too! [*He squirms as if he had the itch.*]

PETER [*beginning to be angry*]: Waal – let him do his own un-hitchin'!

SIMEON [*angry in his turn*]: Let's hustle in an' git our bundles an' be a-goin' as he's a-comin'. I don't want never t' step inside the door agen arter he's back.

[*They both start back around the corner of the house.* EBEN *follows them.*]

EBEN [*anxiously*]: Will ye sign it afore ye go?

PETER: Let's see the colour o' the old skinflint's money an' we'll sign.

[*They disappear left. The two brothers clump upstairs to get their bundles.* EBEN *appears in the kitchen, runs to window, peers out, comes back and pulls up a strip of flooring under stove, takes out a canvas bag and puts it on table, then sets the floor-board back in place. The two brothers appear a moment after. They carry old carpet bags.*]

EBEN [*puts his hand on bag guardingly*]: Have ye signed?

SIMEON [*shows paper in his hand*]: Ay-eh. [*Greedily*] Be that the money?

EBEN [*opens bag and pours out pile of twenty-dollar gold pieces*]: Twenty-dollar pieces – thirty on 'em. Count 'em. [PETER *does so, arranging them in stacks of five, biting one or two to test them.*]

PETER: Six hundred. [*He puts them in bag and puts it inside his shirt carefully.*]

SIMEON [*handing paper to* EBEN]: Har ye be.

EBEN [*after a glance, folds it carefully and hides it under his shirt – gratefully*]: Thank yew.

PETER: Thank yew fur the ride.

SIMEON: We'll send ye a lump o' gold fur Christmas. [*A pause. He stares at them and they at him.*]

PETER [*awkwardly*]: Waal – we're a-goin'.

SIMEON: Comin' out t' the yard?

EBEN: No. I'm waitin' in here a spell. [*Another silence. The brothers edge awkwardly to door in rear – then turn and stand.*]

SIMEON: Waal – good-bye.

PETER: Good-bye.

EBEN: Good-bye.

[*They go out. He sits down at the table, faces the stove, and pulls out the paper. He looks from it to the stove. His face, lighted up by the shaft of sunlight from the window, has an expression of trance. His lips move. The two brothers come out to the gate.*]

PETER [*looking off toward barn*]: Thar he be – unhitchin'.

SIMEON [*with a chuckle*]: I'll bet ye he's riled!

PETER: An' thar she be.

SIMEON: Let's wait 'n' see what our new Maw looks like.

PETER [*with a grin*]: An' give him our partin' cuss!

SIMEON [*grinning*]: I feel like raisin' fun. I feel light in my head an' feet.

PETER: Me, too. I feel like laffin' till I'd split up the middle.

SIMEON: Reckon it's the likker?

PETER: No. My feet feel itchin' t' walk an' walk – an' jump high over thin's – an' –

SIMEON: Dance? [*A pause*]

PETER [*puzzled*]: It's plumb onnateral.

SIMEON [*a light coming over his face*]: I calc'late it's 'cause school's out. It's holiday. Fur once we're free!

PETER [*dazedly*]: Free?

SIMEON: The halter's broke – the harness is busted – the fence bars is down – the stone walls air crumblin' an' tumblin'! We'll be kickin' up an' tearin' away down the road!

PETER [*drawing a deep breath – oratorically*]: Anybody that wants this stinkin' old rock-pile of a farm kin hev it. 'Tain't our'n, no sirree!

SIMEON [*takes the gate off its hinges and puts it under his arm*]: We harby 'bolishes shet gates, an' open gates, an' all gates, by thunder!

PETER: We'll take it with us fur luck an' let 'er sail free down some river.

SIMEON [*as a sound of voices comes from left, rear*]: Har they comes!

[*The two brothers congeal into two stiff, grim-visaged statues.* EPHRAIM CABOT *and* ABBIE PUTNAM *come in.* CABOT *is seventy-five, tall and gaunt, with great, wiry, concentrated power, but stoop-shouldered from toil. His face is as hard as if it were hewn out of a boulder, yet there is a weakness in it, a petty pride in its own narrow strength. His eyes are small, close together, and extremely near-sighted, blinking continually in the effort to focus on objects, their stare having a straining, ingrowing quality. He is dressed in his dismal black Sunday suit.* ABBIE *is thirty-five, buxom, full of vitality. Her round face is pretty, but marred by its rather gross sensuality. There is strength and obstinacy in her jaw, a hard determination in her eyes, and about her whole personality the same unsettled, untamed, desperate quality which is so apparent in* EBEN.]

CABOT [*as they enter – a queer strangled emotion in his dry cracking voice*]: Har we be t' hum, Abbie.

ABBIE [*with lust for the word*]: Hum! [*Her eyes gloating on the house without seeming to see the two stiff figures at the gate.*] It's purty – purty! I can't b'lieve it's r'ally mine.

CABOT [*sharply*]: Yewr'n? Mine! [*He stares at her penetratingly. She stares back. He adds relentingly.*] Our'n – mebbe! It was lonesome too long. I was growin' old in the spring. A hum's got t' hev a woman.

ABBIE [*her voice taking possession*]: A woman's got t' hev a hum!

CABOT [*nodding uncertainly*]: Ay-eh. [*Then irritably*] Whar be they? Ain't thar nobody about – 'r wukin' – 'r nothin'?

ABBIE [*sees the brothers. She returns their stare of cold appraising contempt with interest – slowly*]: Thar's two men loafin' at the gate an' starin' at me like a couple o' strayed hogs.

CABOT [*straining his eyes*]: I kin see 'em – but I can't make out –

SIMEON: It's Simeon.

PETER: It's Peter.

CABOT [*exploding*]: Why hain't ye wukin'?

SIMEON [*dryly*]: We're waitin' t' welcome ye hum – yew an' the bride!

CABOT [*confusedly*]: Hunh? Waal – this be yer new Maw, boys. [*She stares at them and they at her.*]

SIMEON [*turns away and spits contemptuously*]: I see her!

PETER [*spits also*]: An' I see her!

ABBIE [*with the conqueror's conscious superiority*]: I'll go in an' look at *my* house. [*She goes slowly around to porch.*]

SIMEON [*with a snort*]: *Her* house!

PETER [*calls after her*]: Ye'll find Eben inside. Ye better not tell him it's *yewr* house.

ABBIE [*mouthing the name*]: Eben. [*Then quietly*] I'll tell Eben.

CABOT [*with a contemptuous sneer*]: Ye needn't heed Eben. Eben's a dumb fool – like his Maw – soft an' simple!

SIMEON [*with his sardonic burst of laughter*]: Ha! Eben's a chip o' yew – spit 'n' image – hard 'n' bitter's a hickory tree! Dog'll eat dog. He'll eat ye yet, old man!

CABOT [*commandingly*]: Ye git t' wuk!

SIMEON [*as ABBIE disappears in house – winks at PETER and*

says tauntingly]: So that thar's our new Maw, be it? Whar in hell did ye dig her up? [*He and* PETER *laugh.*]

PETER: Ha! Ye'd better turn her in the pen with the other sows. [*They laugh uproariously, slapping their thighs.*]

CABOT [*so amazed at their effrontery that he stutters in confusion*]: Simeon! Peter! What's come over ye? Air ye drunk?

SIMEON: We're free, old man – free o' yew an' the hull damned farm! [*They grow more and more hilarious and excited.*]

PETER: An' we're startin' out fur the gold-fields o' Californi-a!

SIMEON: Ye kin take this place an' burn it!

PETER: An' bury it – fur all we cares!

SIMEON: We're free, old man! [*He cuts a caper.*]

PETER: Free! [*He gives a kick in the air.*]

SIMEON [*in a frenzy*]: Whoop!

PETER: Whoop! [*They do an absurd Indian war dance about the old man, who is petrified between rage and the fear that they are insane.*]

SIMEON: We're free as Injuns! Lucky we don't skulp ye!

PETER: An' burn yer barn an' kill the stock!

SIMEON: An' rape yer new woman! Whoop! [*He and* PETER *stop their dance, holding their sides, rocking with wild laughter.*]

CABOT [*edging away*]: Lust fur gold – fur the sinful, easy gold o' Californi-a! It's made ye mad!

SIMEON [*tauntingly*]: Wouldn't ye like us to send ye back some sinful gold, ye old sinner?

PETER: They's gold besides what's in Californi-a! [*He retreats back beyond the vision of the old man and takes the bag of money and flaunts it in the air about his head, laughing.*]

SIMEON: And sinfuller, too!

PETER: We'll be voyagin' on the sea! Whoop! [*He leaps up and down.*]

SIMEON: Livin' free! Whoop! [*He leaps in turn.*]

CABOT [*suddenly roaring with rage*]: My cuss on ye!

SIMEON: Take our'n in trade fur it! Whoop!

CABOT: I'll hev ye both chained up in the asylum!

PETER: Ye old skinflint! Good-bye!

SIMEON: Ye old blood-sucker! Good-bye!

CABOT: Go afore I – !

PETER: Whoop! [*He picks a stone from the road.* SIMEON *does the same.*]

SIMEON: Maw'll be in the parlour.

PETER: Ay-eh! One! Two!

CABOT [*frightened*]: What air ye – ?

PETER: Three! [*They both throw, the stones hitting the parlour window with a crash of glass, tearing the shade.*]

SIMEON: Whoop!

PETER: Whoop!

CABOT [*in a fury now, rushing toward them*]: If I kin lay hand on ye – I'll break yer bones fur ye!

[*But they beat a capering retreat before him,* SIMEON *with the gate still under his arm.* CABOT *comes back, panting with impotent rage. Their voices as they go off take up the song of the gold-seekers to the old tune of* 'Oh, Susannah!']

> 'I jumped aboard the Liza ship,
> And travelled on the sea,
> And every time I thought of home
> I wished it wasn't me!
> Oh! Californi-a,
> That's the land fur me!
> I'm off to Californi-a!
> With my wash-bowl on my knee.'

[*In the meantime the window of the upper bedroom on right is raised and* ABBIE *sticks her head out. She looks down at* CABOT – *with a sigh of relief.*]

ABBIE: Waal – that's the last o' them two, hain't it? [*He doesn't answer. Then in possessive tones*] This here's a nice bedroom, Ephraim. It's a r'al nice bed. Is it my room, Ephraim?

CABOT [*grimly – without looking up*]: Our'n! [*She cannot control a grimace of aversion and pulls back her head slowly and shuts the window. A sudden horrible thought seems to enter* CABOT's *head.*] They been up to somethin'! Mebbe – mebbe they've pizened the stock – 'r somethin'!

[*He almost runs off down toward the barn. A moment later the kitchen door is slowly pushed open and* ABBIE *enters. For a moment she stands looking at* EBEN. *He does not notice her at first. Her eyes take him in penetratingly with a calculating appraisal of his strength as against hers. But under this her desire is dimly awakened by his youth and good looks. Suddenly he becomes conscious of her presence and looks up. Their eyes meet. He leaps to his feet, glowering at her speechlessly.*]

ABBIE [*in her most seductive tones which she uses all through this scene*]: Be you – Eben? I'm Abbie – [*She laughs.*] I mean, I'm yer new Maw.

EBEN [*viciously*]: No, damn ye!

ABBIE [*as if she hadn't heard – with a queer smile*]: Yer Paw's spoke a lot o' yew –

EBEN: Ha!

ABBIE: Ye mustn't mind him. He's an old man. [*A long pause. They stare at each other.*] I don't want t' pretend playin' Maw t' ye, Eben. [*Admiringly*] Ye're too big an' too strong fur that. I want t' be fren's with ye. Mebbe with me fur a fren' ye'd find ye'd like livin' here better. I kin make it easy fur ye with him, mebbe. [*With a scornful sense of power*] I calc'late I kin git him t' do most anythin' fur me.

EBEN [*with bitter scorn*]: Ha! [*They stare again,* EBEN *obscurely moved, physically attracted to her – in forced stilted tones.*] Yew kin go t' the devil!

ABBIE [*calmly*]: If cussin' me does ye good, cuss all ye've a mind t'. I'm all prepared t' have ye agin me – at fust. I don't blame ye nuther. I'd feel the same at any stranger comin' t' take my Maw's place. [*He shudders. She is watching him carefully.*] Yew must've cared a lot fur yewr Maw, didn't ye? My Maw died afore I'd growed. I don't remember her none. [*A pause*] But yew won't hate me long, Eben. I'm not the wust in the world – an' yew an' me've got a lot in common. I kin tell that by lookin' at ye. Waal – I've had a hard life, too – oceans o' trouble an' nuthin' but wuk fur reward. I was a' orphan early an' had t' wuk fur others in others' hums. Then I married, an' he turned out a drunken spreer an' so he had to wuk for others an' me too agen in others' hums, an' the baby died, an' my husband got sick an' died too, an' I was glad, sayin' now I'm free fur once, on'y I diskivered right away all I was free fur was t' wuk agen in others' hums, doin' others' wuk in others' hums till I'd most give up hope o' ever doin' my own wuk in my own hum, an' then your Paw come –

[CABOT *appears, returning from the barn. He comes to the gate and looks down the road the brothers have gone. A faint strain of their retreating voices is heard;* 'Oh Californi-a! That's the place for me.' *He stands glowering, his fist clenched, his face grim with rage.*]

EBEN [*fighting against his growing attraction and sympathy – harshly*]: An' bought yew – like a harlot! [*She is stung and flushes angrily. She has been sincerely moved by the recital of her troubles. He adds furiously*] An' the price he's payin' ye – this farm – was my Maw's, damn ye! – an' mine now!

ABBIE [*with a cool laugh of confidence*]: Yewr'n? We'll see 'bout that! [*Then strongly*] Waal – what if I did need a hum? What else'd I marry an old man like him fur?

EBEN [*maliciously*]: I'll tell him ye said that!

ABBIE [*smiling*]: I'll say ye're lyin' a-purpose – an' he'll drive ye off the place!

EBEN: Ye devil!

ABBIE [*defying him*]: This be my farm – this be my hum – this be my kitchen –!

EBEN [*furiously, as if he were going to attack her*]: Shut up, damn ye!

ABBIE [*walks up to him – a queer coarse expression of desire in her face and body – slowly*]: An' upstairs – that be my bedroom – an' my bed! [*He stares into her eyes, terribly confused and torn. She adds softly.*] I hain't bad nor mean – 'ceptin' fur an enemy – but I got t' fight fur what's due me out o' life, if I ever 'spect t' git it. [*Then putting her hand on his arm – seductively*] Let's yew 'n' me be fren's, Eben.

EBEN [*stupidly – as if hypnotized*]: Ay-eh. [*Then furiously flinging off her arm*] No, ye durned old witch! I hate ye! [*He rushes out the door.*]

ABBIE [*looks after him, smiling satisfiedly – then half to herself, mouthing the words*]: Eben's nice. [*She looks at the table, proudly.*] I'll wash up *my* dishes now. [EBEN *appears outside, slamming the door behind him. He comes around corner, stops on seeing his father, and stands staring at him with hate.*]

CABOT [*raising his arms to Heaven in the fury he can no longer control*]: Lord God o' Hosts, smite the undutiful sons with Thy wust cuss.

EBEN [*breaking in violently*]: Yew 'n' yewr God! Allus cussin' folks – allus naggin' em!

CABOT [*oblivious to him – summoningly*]: God o' the old! God o' the lonesome!

EBEN [*mockingly*]: Naggin' His sheep t' sin! T' hell with yewr God!

CABOT [*wrathfully*]: 'The days air prolonged and every vision faileth!'

EBEN [*spitting*]: Good enuf fur ye! [CABOT *turns. He and* EBEN *glower at each other.*]

CABOT [*harshly*]: So it's yew. I might've knowed it. [*Shaking his finger threateningly at him*] Blasphemin' fool! [*Then quickly*] Why hain't ye t' wuk?

EBEN: Why hain't yew? They've went. I can't wuk it all alone.

CABOT [*contemptuously*]: Nor noways! I'm wuth ten o' ye yit, old's I be! Ye'll never be more'n half a man! [*Then, matter-of-factly*] Waal – let's git t' the barn.

[*They go. A last faint note of the 'Californi-a' song is heard from the distance.* ABBIE *is washing the dishes.*]

CURTAIN

PART TWO

SCENE 1

The exterior of the farm-house, as in Part One – a hot Sunday afternoon two months later.

[ABBIE, *dressed in her best, is discovered sitting in a rocker at the end of the porch. She rocks listlessly, enervated by the heat, staring in front of her with bored, half-closed eyes.*

EBEN *sticks his head out of his bedroom window. He looks around furtively and tries to see – or hear – if anyone is on the porch, but although he has been careful to make no noise,* ABBIE *has sensed his movement. She stops rocking, her face grows animated and eager, she waits attentively.* EBEN *seems to feel her presence, he scowls back his thoughts of her and spits with exaggerated disdain – then withdraws back into the room.* ABBIE *waits, holding her breath as she listens with passionate eagerness for every sound within the house.*

EBEN *comes out. Their eyes meet. His falter, he is confused, he turns away and slams the door resentfully. At this gesture,* ABBIE *laughs tantalizingly, amused, but at the same time piqued and irritated. He scowls, strides off the porch to the path and starts to walk past her to the road with a grand swagger of ignoring her existence. He is dressed in his store suit, spruced up, his face shines from soap and water.* ABBIE *leans forward on her chair, her eyes hard and angry now, and, as he passes her, gives a sneering, taunting chuckle.*]

EBEN [*stung – turns on her furiously*]: What air yew cacklin' 'bout?
ABBIE [*triumphant*]: Yew!
EBEN: What about me?

ABBIE: Ye look all slicked up like a prize bull.

EBEN [*with a sneer*]: Waal – ye hain't so durned purty yerself, be ye? [*They stare into each other's eyes, his held by hers in spite of himself, hers glowingly possessive. Their physical attraction becomes a palpable force quivering in the hot air.*]

ABBIE [*softly*]: Ye don't mean that, Eben. Ye may think ye mean it, mebbe, but ye don't. Ye can't. It's agin nature, Eben. Ye been fightin' yer nature ever since the day I come – tryin' t' tell yerself I hain't purty t' ye. [*She laughs a low humid laugh without taking her eyes from his. A pause – her body squirms desirously – she murmurs languorously*] Hain't the sun strong an' hot? Ye kin feel it burnin' into the earth – Nature – makin' thin's grow – bigger 'n' bigger – burnin' inside ye – makin' ye want t' grow – into somethin' else – till ye're jined with it – an' it's your'n – but it owns ye, too – an' makes ye grow bigger – like a tree – like them elums – [*She laughs again softly, holding his eyes. He takes a step toward her, compelled against his will.*] Nature'll beat ye, Eben. Ye might's well own up t' it fust 's last.

EBEN [*trying to break from her spell – confusedly*]: If Paw'd hear ye goin' on . . . [*Resentfully*] But ye've made such a damned idjit out o' the old devil . . . [ABBIE *laughs.*]

ABBIE: Waal – hain't it easier fur yew with him changed softer?

EBEN [*defiantly*]: No. I'm fightin' him – fightin' yew – fightin' fur Maw's rights t' her hum! [*This breaks her spell for him. He glowers at her.*] An' I'm on to ye. Ye hain't foolin' me a mite. Ye're aimin' t' swaller up everythin' an' make it your'n. Waal, you'll find I'm a heap sight bigger hunk nor yew kin chew! [*He turns from her with a sneer.*]

ABBIE [*trying to regain her ascendancy – seductively*]: Eben!

EBEN: Leave me be! [*He starts to walk away.*]

ABBIE [*more commandingly*]: Eben!

EBEN [*stops – resentfully*]: What d'ye want?

ABBIE [*trying to conceal a growing excitement*]: Whar air ye goin'?

EBEN [*with malicious nonchalance*]: Oh – up the road a spell.

ABBIE: T' the village?

EBEN [*airily*]: Mebbe.

ABBIE [*excitedly*]: T' see that Min, I s'pose?

EBEN: Mebbe.

ABBIE [*weakly*]: What d'ye want t' waste time on her fur?

EBEN [*revenging himself now – grinning at her*]: Ye can't beat Nature, didn't ye say? [*He laughs and again starts to walk away.*]

ABBIE [*bursting out*]: An ugly old hake!

EBEN [*with a tantalizing sneer*]: She's purtier'n yew be!

ABBIE: That every wuthless drunk in the country has . . .

EBEN [*tauntingly*]: Mebbe – but she's better'n yew. She owns up fa'r 'n' squar' t' her doin's.

ABBIE [*furiously*]: Don't ye dare compare –

EBEN: She don't go sneakin' an' stealin' – what's mine.

ABBIE [*savagely seizing on his weak point*]: Your'n? Yew mean – my farm?

EBEN: I mean the farm yew sold yerself fur like any other old whore – my farm!

ABBIE [*stung – fiercely*]: Ye'll never live t' see the day when even a stinkin' weed on it 'll belong t' ye! [*Then in a scream*] Git out o' my sight! Go on t' yer slut – disgracin' yer Paw 'n' me! I'll git yer Paw t' horsewhip ye off the place if I want t'! Ye're only livin' here 'cause I tolerate ye! Git along! I hate the sight o' ye! [*She stops, panting and glaring at him.*]

EBEN [*returning her glance in kind*]: An' I hate the sight o' yew! [*He turns and strides off up the road. She follows his retreating figure with concentrated hate. Old CABOT appears coming up from the barn. The hard, grim expression of his face has changed. He seems in some queer way softened, mellowed. His eyes have taken on a strange, incongruous dreamy quality. Yet there is no hint of physical weakness about him – rather he looks more robust and younger. ABBIE sees him and turns*] *away quickly with unconcealed aversion. He comes slowly up to her.*]

CABOT [*mildly*]: War yew an' Eben quarrellin' agin?

ABBIE [*shortly*]: No.

CABOT: Ye was talkin' a'mighty loud. . . . [*He sits down on the edge of porch.*]

ABBIE [*snappishly*]: If ye heerd us they hain't no need askin' questions.

CABOT: I didn't hear what ye said.

ABBIE [*relieved*]: Waal – it wa'n't nothin' t' speak on.

CABOT [*after a pause*]: Eben's queer.

ABBIE [*bitterly*]: He's the dead spit 'n' image o' yew!

CABOT [*queerly interested*]: D'ye think so, Abbie? [*After a pause, ruminatingly*] Me 'n' Eben's allus fit 'n' fit. I never could b'ar him noways. He's so thunderin' soft – like his Maw.

ABBIE [*scornfully*]: Ay-eh! 'Bout as soft as yew be!

CABOT [*as if he hadn't heard*]: Mebbe I been too hard on him.

ABBIE [*jeeringly*]: Waal – ye're gittin' soft now – soft as slop! That's what Eben was sayin'.

CABOT [*his face instantly grim and ominous*]: Eben was sayin'? Waal, he'd best not do nothin' t' try me 'r he'll soon diskiver . . . [*A pause. She keeps her face turned away. His gradually softens. He stares up at the sky.*] Purty, hain't it?

ABBIE [*crossly*]: I don't see nothin' purty.

CABOT: The sky. Feels like a warm field up thar.

ABBIE [*sarcastically*]: Air yew aimin' t' buy up over the farm, too? [*She snickers contemptuously.*]

CABOT [*strangely*]: I'd like t' own my place up thar. [*A pause*] I'm getting old, Abbie. I'm gittin' ripe on the bough. [*A pause. She stares at him mystified. He goes on.*] It's allus lonesome cold in the house – even when it's bilin' hot outside. Hain't yew noticed?

ABBIE: No.

CABOT: It's warm down t' the barn – nice smellin' an' warm – with the cows. [*A pause*] Cows is queer.

ABBIE: Like yew!

CABOT: Like Eben. [*A pause*] I'm gittin' t' feel resigned t' Eben – jest as I got t' feel 'bout his Maw. I'm gittin' t' learn to b'ar his softness – jest like her'n. I calc'late I c'd a'most take t' him – if he wa'n't sech a dumb fool! [*A pause*] I s'pose it's old age a-creepin' in my bones.

ABBIE [*indifferently*]: Waal – ye hain't dead yet.

CABOT [*roused*]: No, I hain't, yew bet – not by a hell of a sight – I'm sound 'n' tough as hickory! [*Then moodily*] But arter three score and ten the Lord warns ye t' prepare. [*A pause*] That's why Eben's come in my head. Now that his cussed sinful brothers is gone their path t' hell, they's no one left but Eben.

ABBIE [*resentfully*]: They's me, hain't they? [*Agitatedly*] What's all this sudden likin' ye've tuk to Eben? Why don't ye say nothin' 'bout me? Hain't I yer lawful wife?

CABOT [*simply*]: Ay-eh. Ye be. [*A pause – he stares at her desirously – his eyes grow avid – then with a sudden movement he seizes her hands and squeezes them, declaiming in a queer camp-meeting preacher's tempo.*] Yew air my Rose o' Sharon! Behold, yew air fair; yer eyes air doves; yer lips air like scarlet; yer two breasts air like two fawns; yer navel be like a round goblet; yer belly be like a heap o' wheat . . . [*He covers her hand with kisses. She does not seem to notice. She stares before her with hard angry eyes.*]

ABBIE [*jerking her hands away – harshly*]: So ye're plannin' t' leave the farm t' Eben, air ye?

CABOT [*dazedly*]: Leave . . .? [*Then with resentful obstinacy*] I hain't a-givin' it t' no one!

ABBIE [*remorselessly*]: Ye can't take it with ye.

CABOT [*thinks a moment – then reluctantly*]: No, I calc'late not. [*After a pause – with a strange passion*] But if I could, I would, by the Etarnal! 'R if I could, in my dyin' hour, I'd set it afire an' watch it burn – this house an' every ear o' corn an' every tree down t' the last blade o' hay! I'd sit an' know it was all a–dying with me an' no one else'd ever own what was mine, what I'd made out o' nothin' with my own sweat 'n' blood! [*A pause – then he adds with a queer affection.*] 'Ceptin' the cows. Them I'd turn free.

ABBIE [*harshly*]: An' me?

CABOT [*with a queer smile*]: Ye'd be turned free, too.

ABBIE [*furiously*]: So that's the thanks I git fur marryin' ye – t' have ye change kind to Eben who hates ye, an' talk o' turnin' me out in the road.

CABOT [*hastily*]: Abbie! Ye know I wa'n't. . . .

ABBIE [*vengefully*]: Just let me tell ye a thing or two 'bout Eben! Whar's he gone? T' see that harlot, Min! I tried fur t' stop him. Disgracin' yew an' me – on the Sabbath, too!

CABOT [*rather guiltily*]: He's a sinner – nateral-born. It's lust eatin' his heart.

ABBIE [*enraged beyond endurance – wildly vindictive*]: An' his lust fur me! Kin ye find excuses fur that?

CABOT [*stares at her – after a dead pause*]: Lust – fur yew?

ABBIE [*defiantly*]: He was tryin' t' make love t' me – when ye heerd us quarrellin'.

CABOT [*stares at her – then a terrible expression of rage comes over his face – he springs to his feet shaking all over*]: By the A'mighty God – I'll end him!

ABBIE [*frightened now for* EBEN]: No! Don't ye!

CABOT [*violently*]: I'll git the shotgun an' blow his soft brains t' the top o' them elums!

ABBIE [*throwing her arms around him*]: No, Ephraim!

CABOT [*pushing her away violently*]: I will, by God!

ABBIE [*in a quieting tone*]: Listen, Ephraim. T'wa'n't nothin' bad – on'y a boy's foolin' – t'wa'n't meant serious – jest jokin' an' teasin' . . .

CABOT: Then why did ye say – lust?

ABBIE: It must hev sounded wusser'n I meant. An' I was mad at thinkin' – ye'd leave him the farm.

CABOT [*quieter, but still grim and cruel*]: Waal then, I'll horse-whip him off the place if that much'll content ye.

ABBIE [*reaching out and taking his hand*]: No. Don't think o' me! Ye mustn't drive him off. T'ain't sensible. Who'll ye get to help ye on the farm? They's no one hereabouts.

CABOT [*considers this – then nodding his appreciation*]: Ye got a head on ye. [*Then irritably*] Waal, let him stay. [*He sits down on the edge of the porch. She sits beside him. He murmurs contemptuously.*] I oughtn't t' git riled so – at that 'ere fool calf. [*A pause*] But har's the p'int. What son o' mine'll keep on here t' the farm – when the Lord does call me? Simeon an' Peter air gone t' hell – an Eben's follerin' 'em –

ABBIE: They's me.

CABOT: Ye're on'y a woman.

ABBIE: I'm yewr wife.

CABOT: That hain't me. A son is me – my blood – mine. Mine ought t' git mine. An' then it's still mine – even though I be six foot under. D'ye see?

ABBIE [*giving him a look of hatred*]: Ay-eh. I see. [*She becomes very thoughtful, her face growing shrewd, her eyes studying* CABOT *craftily.*]

CABOT: I'm gittin' old – ripe on the bough. [*Then with a sudden forced reassurance*] Not but what I hain't a hard nut t' crack even yet – an' fur many a year t' come! By the Etarnal, I kin break most o' the young fellers' backs at any kind o' work any day o' the year!

ABBIE [*suddenly*]: Mebbe the Lord'll give *us* a son.

CABOT [*turns and stares at her eagerly*]: Ye mean – a son – t' me 'n' yew?

ABBIE [*with a cajoling smile*]: Ye're a strong man yet, hain't ye? 'Tain't noways impossible, be it? We know that. Why d'ye stare so? Hain't ye never thought o' that afore? I been thinkin' o' it all along. Ay-eh – an' I been prayin' it'd happen, too.

CABOT [*his face growing full of joyous pride and a sort of religious ecstasy*]: Ye been prayin', Abbie? – fur a son? – t' us?

ABBIE: Ay-eh. [*With a grim resolution*] I want a son now.

CABOT [*excitedly clutching both of her hands in his*]: It'd be the blessin' o' God, Abbie – the blessin' o' God A'mighty on me – in my old age – in my lonesomeness! They hain't nothin' I wouldn't do fur ye then, Abbie. Ye'd hev on'y ask it – anythin' ye'd a mind t' –

ABBIE [*interrupting*]: Would ye will the farm t' me then – t' me an' it – ?

CABOT [*vehemently*]: I'd do anythin' ye axed, I tell ye! I swear it! May I be everlastin' damned t' hell if I wouldn't! [*He sinks to his knees, pulling her down with him. He trembles all over with the fervour of his hopes.*] Pray t' the Lord agin, Abbie. It's the Sabbath! I'll jine ye! Two prayers air better nor one. 'An' God hearkened unto Rachel an' she conceived an' bore a son.' An' God hearkened unto Abbie! Pray, Abbie! Pray fur Him to hearken! [*He bows his head, mumbling. She pretends to do likewise, but gives him a side glance of scorn and triumph.*]

SCENE 2

About eight in the evening. The interior of the two bedrooms on the top floor is shown.

[EBEN *is sitting on the side of his bed in the room on the left. On account of the heat he has taken off everything but his undershirt and pants. His feet are bare. He faces front, brooding moodily, his chin propped on his hands, a desperate expression on his face.*

In the other room CABOT *and* ABBIE *are sitting side by side on the edge of their bed, an old fourposter with feather mattress. He is in his nightshirt, she in her nightdress. He is still in the queer excited mood into which the notion of a son has thrown him. Both rooms are lighted dimly and flickeringly by tallow candles.*]

CABOT: The farm needs a son.

ABBIE: I need a son.

CABOT: Ay-eh. Sometimes ye air the farm an' sometimes the farm be yew. That's why I clove t' ye in my lonesomeness. [*A pause. He pounds his knee with his fist.*] Me an' the farm has got t' beget a son!

ABBIE: Ye'd best go t' sleep. Ye're gittin' thin's all mixed.

CABOT [*with an impatient gesture*]: No, I hain't. My mind's clear's a well. Ye don't know me, that's it. [*He stares hopelessly at the floor.*]

ABBIE [*indifferently*]: Mebbe.

[*In the next room* EBEN *gets up and paces up and down distractedly.* ABBIE *hears him. Her eyes fasten on the intervening wall with concentrated attention.* EBEN *stops and stares. Their hot glances seem to meet through the wall. Unconsciously he stretches out his arms for her and she half-rises. Then aware, he mutters a curse at himself and flings himself face downward on the bed, his clenched fists above his head, his face buried in the pillow.* ABBIE *relaxes with a faint sigh, but her eyes remain fixed on the wall, she listens with all her attention for some movement from* EBEN.]

CABOT [*suddenly raises his head and looks at her – scornfully*]: Will ye ever know me – 'r will any man 'r woman? [*Shaking his head*] No. I calc'late 't wa'n't t' be. [*He turns away.* ABBIE *looks at the wall. Then, evidently unable to keep silent about his thoughts, without looking at his wife, he puts out his hand and clutches her knee. She starts violently, looks at him, sees he is not watching her, concentrates again on the wall and pays no attention to what he says.*] Listen, Abbie. When I come here fifty-odd year ago – I was jest twenty an' the strongest an' hardest ye ever seen – ten times as strong an' fifty times as hard as Eben. Waal – this place was nothin' but fields o' stones. Folks laughed when I tuk it. They couldn't know what I knowed. When ye kin make corn sprout out o' stones, God's livin' in yew. They wa'n't strong enuf fur that! They reckoned God was easy. They laughed. They don't laugh no more. Some died hereabouts. Some went West an' died. They're all under ground – fur follerin' arter an easy God. God hain't easy. [*He shakes his head slowly.*] An' I growed hard. Folks kept allus sayin', 'He's a hard man,' like 'twas sinful t' be hard, so's at last I said back at 'em, 'Waal then, by thunder, ye'll git me hard an' see how ye like it!' [*Then suddenly*] But I give in t' weakness once. 'Twas arter I'd been here two year. I got weak – despairful – they was so many stones. They was a party leavin', givin' up, goin' West. I jined 'em. We tracked on 'n' on. We come t' broad medders, plains, whar the soil was black an' rich as gold. Nary a stone. Easy. Ye'd on'y to plough an' sow an' then set an' smoke yer pipe an' watch thin's grow. I could o' been a rich man – but somethin' in me fit me an' fit me – the voice o' God sayin', 'This hain't wuth nothin' t' Me. Git ye back t' hum!' I got afeered o' that voice an' I lit out back t' hum here, leavin' my claim an' crops t' whoever'd a mind t' take 'em. Ay-eh. I actooly give up what was rightful mine! God's hard, not easy! God's in the stones! Build My church on a rock – out o' stones an' I'll be in them! That's what He meant t' Peter! [*He sighs heavily – a pause*] Stones. I picked 'em up an' piled 'em into walls. Ye kin read the years o' my life in them walls, every day a hefted stone, climbin' over the hills up and down, fencing in the fields that was mine, whar I'd made thin's grow out o' nothin' – like the will o' God, like the servant o' His hand. It wa'n't easy. It was hard an' He made me hard fur it. [*He pauses.*] All the time I kept gittin' lonesomer. I tuk a wife. She bore Simeon an' Peter. She was a good woman. She wuked hard. We was married twenty year. She never knowed me. She helped, but she never knowed what she was helpin'. I was allus lonesome. She died. After that it wa'n't so lonesome fur a spell. [*A pause*] I lost count o' the years. I had no time t' fool away countin' 'em. Sim an' Peter helped. The farm growed. It was all mine! When I thought o' that I didn't feel lonesome. [*A pause*] But ye can't hitch yer mind t' one thin' day an' night. I tuk another wife – Eben's Maw. Her folks was contestin' me at law over my deeds t' the farm – my farm! That's why Eben keeps a-talkin' his fool talk o' this bein' his Maw's farm. She bore Eben. She was purty – but soft. She tried t' be hard. She couldn't. She never knowed me nor nothin'. It was lonesomer 'n hell with her. After a matter o' sixteen-odd years, she died. [*A pause*] I lived with the boys. They hated me 'cause I was hard. I hated them 'cause they was soft. They coveted the farm without knowin' what it meant. It made me bitter 'n wormwood. It aged me – them coveting what I'd made fur mine. Then this spring the call come – the voice o' God cryin' in my wilderness, in my lonesomeness – t' go out an' seek an' find! [*Turning to her with strange passion*] I sought ye an' I found ye! Yew air my Rose o' Sharon! Yer eyes air like . . . [*She has turned a blank face, resentful eyes to his. He stares at her for a moment – then harshly*] Air ye any the wiser fur all I've told ye?

ABBIE [*confusedly*]: Mebbe.

CABOT [*pushing her away from him – angrily*]: Ye don't know nothin' – nor never will. If ye don't hev a son t' redeem ye . . . [*This in a tone of cold threat*]

ABBIE [*resentfully*]: I've prayed, hain't I?

CABOT [*bitterly*]: Pray agin – fur understandin'!

ABBIE [*a veiled threat in her tone*]: Ye'll have a son out o' me I promise ye.

CABOT: How can ye promise?

ABBIE: I got second-sight, mebbe. I kin foretell. [*She gives a queer smile.*]

CABOT: I believe ye have. Ye give me the chills sometimes. [*He shivers.*] It's cold in this house. It's oneasy. They's thin's pokin' about in the dark – in the corners. [*He pulls on his trousers, tucking in his night-shirt, and pulls on his boots.*]

ABBIE [*surprised*]: Whar air ye goin'?

CABOT [*queerly*]: Down whar it's restful – whar it's warm – down t' the barn. [*Bitterly*] I kin talk t' the cows. They know. They know the farm an' me. They'll give me peace. [*He turns to go out the door*]

ABBIE [*a bit frightenedly*]: Air ye ailin' tonight, Ephraim?

CABOT: Growin'. Growin' ripe on the bough. [*He turns and goes, his boots clumping down the stairs.* EBEN *sits up with a start, listening.* ABBIE *is conscious of his movement and stares at the wall.* CABOT *comes out of the house around the corner and stands by the gate, blinking at the sky. He stretches up his hands in a tortured gesture.*] God A'mighty, call from the dark!

[*He listens as if expecting an answer. Then his arms drop, he shakes his head and plods off toward the barn.* EBEN *and* ABBIE *stare at each other through the wall.* EBEN *sighs heavily and* ABBIE *echoes it. Both become terribly nervous, uneasy. Finally* ABBIE *gets up and listens, her ear to the wall. He acts as if he saw every move she was making; he becomes resolutely still. She seems driven into a decision – goes out the door in rear determinedly. His eyes follow her. Then as the door of his room is opened softly, he turns away, waits in an attitude of strained fixity.* ABBIE *stands for a second staring at him, her eyes burning with desire. Then with a little cry she runs over and throws her arms about his neck, she pulls his head back and covers his mouth with kisses. At first, he submits dumbly; then he puts his arms about her neck and returns her kisses, but finally, suddenly aware of his hatred, he hurls her away from him, springing to his feet. They stand speechless and breathless, panting like two animals.*]

ABBIE [*at last – painfully*]: Ye shouldn't, Eben – ye shouldn't –
I'd make ye happy!

EBEN [*harshly*]: I don't want happy – from yew!

ABBIE [*helplessly*]: Ye do, Eben! Ye do! Why d'ye lie?

EBEN [*viciously*]: I don't take t' ye, I tell ye! I hate the sight o'
ye!

ABBIE [*with an uncertain troubled laugh*]: Waal, I kissed ye anyways – an' ye kissed back – yer lips was burnin' – ye can't
lie 'bout that! [*Intensely*] If ye don't care, why did ye kiss
me back – why was yer lips burnin'?

EBEN [*wiping his mouth*]: It was like pizen on 'em. [*Then
tauntingly*] When I kissed ye back, mebbe I thought 'twas
someone else.

ABBIE [*wildly*]: Min?

EBEN: Mebbe.

ABBIE [*torturedly*]: Did ye go t' see her? Did ye r'ally go? I
thought ye mightn't. Is that why ye throwed me off jest
now?

EBEN [*sneeringly*]: What if it be?

ABBIE [*raging*]: Then ye're a dog, Eben Cabot!

EBEN [*threateningly*]: Ye can't talk that way t' me!

ABBIE [*with a shrill laugh*]: Can't I? Did ye think I was in love
with ye – a weak thin' like yew? Not much! I on'y wanted
ye fur a purpose o' my own – an' I'll hev ye fur it yet 'cause
I'm stronger'n yew be!

EBEN [*resentfully*]: I knowed well it was on'y part o' yer plan
t' swaller everythin'!

ABBIE [*tauntingly*]: Mebbe!

EBEN [*furious*]: Git out o' my room!

ABBIE: This air my room an' ye're on'y hired help!

EBEN [*threateningly*]: Git out afore I murder ye!

ABBIE [*quite confident now*]: I hain't a mite afeerd. Ye want me,
don't ye? Yes, ye do! An yer Paw's son'll never kill what he
wants! Look at yer eyes! They's lust fur me in 'em, burnin'
'em up! Look at yer lips now! They're tremblin' an' longin'

t' kiss me, an' yer teeth t' bite! [*He is watching her now with a horrible fascination. She laughs a crazy triumphant laugh.*] I'm a-goin' t' make all o' this hum my hum! They's one room hain't mine yet, but it's a-goin' t' be tonight. I'm a-goin' down now an' light up! [*She makes him a mocking bow.*] Won't ye come courtin' me in the best parlour, Mister Cabot?

EBEN [*staring at her – horribly confused – dully*]: Don't ye dare! It hain't been opened since Maw died an' was laid out thar! Don't ye . . . [*But her eyes are fixed on his so burningly that his will seems to wither before hers. He stands swaying toward her helplessly.*]

ABBIE [*holding his eyes and putting all her will into her words as she backs out the door*]: I'll expect ye afore long, Eben.

EBEN [*stares after her for a while, walking toward the door. A light appears in the parlour window. He murmurs*]: In the parlour? [*This seems to arouse connexions, for he comes back and puts on his white shirt, collar, half-ties the tie mechanically, puts on coat, takes his hat, stands barefooted looking about him in bewilderment, mutters wonderingly.*] Maw! Whar air yew? [*Then goes slowly toward the door in rear.*]

SCENE 3

A few minutes later. The interior of the parlour is shown. A grim, repressed room like a tomb in which the family has been interred alive.

[ABBIE *sits on the edge of the horsehair sofa. She has lighted all the candles and the room is revealed in all its preserved ugliness. A change has come over the woman. She looks awed and frightened now, ready to run away.*

The door is opened and EBEN *appears. His face wears an expression of obsessed confusion. He stands staring at her, his arms hanging disjointedly from his shoulders, his feet bare, his hat in his hand.*]

ABBIE [*after a pause – with a nervous, formal politeness*]: Won't ye set?

EBEN [*dully*]: Ay-eh. [*Mechanically he places his hat carefully on the floor near the door and sits stiffly beside her on the edge of the sofa. A pause. They both remain rigid, looking straight ahead with eyes full of fear.*]

ABBIE: When I fust come in – in the dark – they seemed somethin' here.

EBEN [*simply*]: Maw.

ABBIE: I kin still feel – somethin' –

EBEN: It's Maw.

ABBIE: At fust I was feered o' it. I wanted t' yell an' run. Now – since yew come – seems like it's growin' soft an' kind t' me. [*Addressing the air – queerly*] Thank yew.

EBEN: Maw allus loved me.

ABBIE: Mebbe it knows I love ye, too. Mebbe that makes it kind t' me.

EBEN [*dully*]: I dunno. I should think she'd hate ye.

ABBIE [*with certainty*]: No. I kin feel it don't – not no more.

EBEN: Hate ye fur stealin' her place – here in her hum – settin' in her parlour whar she was laid. . . . [*He suddenly stops, staring stupidly before him.*]

ABBIE: What is it, Eben?

EBEN [*in a whisper*]: Seems like Maw didn't want me t' remind ye.

ABBIE [*excitedly*]: I knowed, Eben! It's kind t' me. It don't b'ar me no grudges fur what I never knowed an' couldn't help!

EBEN: Maw b'ars him a grudge.

ABBIE: Waal, so does all o' us.

EBEN: Ay-eh. [*With passion*] I does, by God!

ABBIE [*taking one of his hands in hers and patting it*]: Thar!
Don't git riled thinkin' o' him. Think o' yer Maw who's
kind t' us. Tell me about yer Maw, Eben.

EBEN: They hain't nothin' much. . . . She was kind. She was
good.

ABBIE [*putting one arm over his shoulder. He does not seem to
notice – passionately*]: I'll be kind an' good t' ye!

EBEN: Sometimes she used t' sing fur me.

ABBIE: I'll sing fur ye!

EBEN: This was her hum. This was her farm.

ABBIE: This is my hum. This is my farm.

EBEN: He married her t' steal 'em. She was soft an' easy. He
couldn't 'preciate her.

ABBIE: He can't 'preciate me!

EBEN: He murdered her with his hardness.

ABBIE: He's murderin' me!

EBEN: She died. [*A pause*] Sometimes she used to sing fur me.
[*He bursts into a fit of sobbing.*]

ABBIE [*both her arms around him – with wild passion*]: I'll sing
fur ye! I'll die fur ye! [*In spite of her overwhelming desire for
him, there is a sincere maternal love in her manner and voice – a
horribly frank mixture of lust and mother-love.*] Don't cry,
Eben! I'll take yer Maw's place! I'll be everythin' she was t'
ye! Let me kiss ye, Eben! [*She pulls his head around. He makes
a bewildered pretence of resistance. She is tender.*] Don't be
afeered! I'll kiss ye pure, Eben – same 's if I was a Maw t' ye
– an' ye kin kiss me back 's if yew was my son – my boy –
sayin' good night t' me! Kiss me, Eben. [*They kiss in re-
strained fashion. Then suddenly wild passion overcomes her. She
kisses him lustfully again and again and he flings his arms about
her and returns her kisses. Suddenly, as in the bedroom, he frees
himself from her violently and springs to his feet. He is trembling
all over, in a strange state of terror. ABBIE strains her arms toward
him with fierce pleading.*] Don't ye leave me, Eben! Can't ye
see it hain't enuf – lovin' ye like a Maw – can't ye see it's

got t' be that an' more – much more – a hundred times more
– fur me t' be happy – fur yew t' be happy?

EBEN [*to the presence he feels in the room*]: Maw! Maw! What
d'ye want? What air ye tellin' me?

ABBIE: She's tellin' ye t' love me. She knows I love ye an' I'll
be good t' ye. Can't ye feel it? Don't ye know? She's tellin
ye t' love me, Eben!

EBEN: Ay-eh. I feel – mebbe she – but – I can't figger out –
why – when ye've stole her place – here in her hum – in the
parlour whar she was . . .

ABBIE [*fiercely*]: She knows I love ye!

EBEN [*his face suddenly lighting up with a fierce triumphant grin*]:
I see it! I sees why. It's her vengeance on him – so's she kin
rest quiet in her grave!

ABBIE [*wildly*]: Vengeance o' her on him! Vengeance o' her
on me – an' mine on yew – an' yourn on me – an' ourn on
him! Vengeance o' God on the hull o' us! What d' we give
a durn? I love ye, Eben! God knows I love ye! [*She stretches
out her arms for him.*]

EBEN [*throws himself on his knees beside the sofa and grabs her in
his arms – releasing all his pent-up passion*]: An' I love yew,
Abbie! – now I kin say it! I been dyin' fur want o' ye – every
hour – since ye come! I love ye! [*Their lips meet in a fierce,
bruising kiss.*]

SCENE 4

Exterior of the farm-house. It is just dawn.

    [*The front door at right is opened and* EBEN *comes out and
walks around to the gate. He is dressed in his working clothes.
He seems changed. His face wears a bold and confident expression, he is grinning to himself with evident satisfaction. As he*

gets near the gate, the window of the parlour is heard opening and the shutters are flung back and ABBIE *sticks her head out. Her hair tumbles over her shoulders in disarray, her face is flushed, she looks at* EBEN *with tender, languorous eyes and calls softly.*]

ABBIE: Eben. [*As he turns – playfully*] Jest one more kiss afore ye go. I'm goin' t' miss ye fearful all day.

EBEN: An me yew, ye kin bet! [*He goes to her. They kiss several times. He draws away, laughingly.*] Thar. That's enuf, hain't it? Ye won't hev none left fur next time.

ABBIE: I got a million 'on 'em left fur ye! [*Then a bit anxiously*] D'ye r'ally love me, Eben?

EBEN [*emphatically*]: I like ye better'n any gal I ever knowed! That's gospel!

ABBIE: Likin' hain't lovin'.

EBEN: Waal then – I love ye. Now air yew satisfied?

ABBIE: Ay-eh, I be. [*She smiles at him adoringly.*]

EBEN: I better git t' the barn. The old critter's liable t' suspicion an' come sneakin' up.

ABBIE [*with a confident laugh*]: Let him! I kin allus pull the wool over his eyes. I'm goin' t' leave the shutters open and let in the sun 'n' air. This room's been dead long enuf. Now it's goin' t' be my room.

EBEN [*frowning*]: Ay-eh.

ABBIE [*hastily*]: I meant – our room.

EBEN: Ay-eh.

ABBIE: We made it our'n last night, didn't we? We give it life – our lovin' did. [*A pause*]

EBEN [*with a strange look*]: Maw's gone back t' her grave. She kin sleep now.

ABBIE: May she rest in peace! [*Then tenderly rebuking*] Ye oughtn't t' talk o' sad thin's – this mornin'.

EBEN: It jest come up in my mind o' itself.

ABBIE: Don't let it. [*He doesn't answer. She yawns.*] Waal, I'm

a-goin' t' steal a wink o' sleep. I'll tell the Old Man I hain't
feelin' pert. Let him git his own vittles.

EBEN: I see him comin' from the barn. Ye better look smart an'
git upstairs.

ABBIE: Ay-eh. Good-bye. Don't ferget me.

[*She throws him a kiss. He grins – then squares his shoulders
and awaits his father confidently.* CABOT *walks slowly up
from the left, staring up at the sky with a vague face.*]

EBEN [*jovially*]: Mornin', Paw. Star-gazin' in daylight?

CABOT: Purty, hain't it?

EBEN [*looking around him possessively*]: It's a durned purty farm.

CABOT: I mean the sky.

EBEN [*grinning*]: How d'ye know? Them eyes o' your'n can't
see that fur. [*This tickles his humour and he slaps his thigh and
laughs.*] Ho-ho! That's a good un!

CABOT [*grimly sarcastic*]: Ye're feelin' right chipper, hain't ye?
Whar'd ye steal the likker?

EBEN [*good-naturedly*]: 'Tain't likker. Jest life. [*Suddenly holding
out his hand – soberly*] Yew 'n' me is quits. Let's shake
hands.

CABOT [*suspiciously*]: What's come over ye?

EBEN: Then don't. Mebbe it's jest as well. [*A moment's pause*]
What's come over me? [*Queerly*] Didn't ye feel her passin'
– goin' back t' her grave?

CABOT [*dully*]: Who?

EBEN: Maw. She kin rest now an' sleep content. She's quits
with ye.

CABOT [*confusedly*]: I rested. I slept good – down with the
cows. They know how t' sleep. They're teachin' me.

EBEN [*suddenly jovial again*]: Good fur the cows! Waal – ye
better git t' work.

CABOT [*grimly amused*]: Air yew bossin' me, ye calf?

EBEN [*beginning to laugh*]: Ay-eh! I'm bossin' yew! Ha-ha-ha!
See how ye like it! Ha-ha-ha! I'm the prize rooster o' this
roost. Ha-ha-ha! [*He goes off toward the barn laughing.*]

CABOT [*looks after him with scornful pity*]: Soft-headed. Like his Maw. Dead spit 'n' image. No hope in him! [*He spits with contemptuous disgust.*] A born fool! [*Then matter-of-factly*] Waal – I'm gittin' peckish. [*He goes toward door.*]

PART THREE

SCENE 1

A night in late spring the following year. The kitchen and the two bedrooms upstairs are shown. The two bedrooms are dimly lighted by a tallow candle in each.

[EBEN *is sitting on the side of the bed in his room, his chin propped on his fists, his face a study of the struggle he is making to understand his conflicting emotions. The noisy laughter and music from below where a kitchen dance is in progress annoy and distract him. He scowls at the floor.*

In the next room a cradle stands beside the double bed.

In the kitchen all is festivity. The stove has been taken down to give more room to the dancers. The chairs, with wooden benches added, have been pushed back against the walls. On these are seated, squeezed in tight against one another, farmers and their wives and their young folks of both sexes from the neighbouring farms. They are all chattering and laughing loudly. They evidently have some secret joke in common. There is no end of winking, of nudging, of meaning nods of the head toward CABOT *who, in a state of extreme hilarious excitement increased by the amount he has drunk, is standing near the rear door where there is a small keg of whisky and serving drinks to all the men. In the left corner, front, dividing the attention with her husband,* ABBIE *is sitting in a rocking chair, a shawl wrapped about her shoulders. She is very pale, her face is thin and drawn, her eyes are fixed anxiously on the open door in rear as if waiting for someone.*

The musician is tuning up his fiddle, seated in the far right corner. He is a lanky young fellow with a long weak face. His

*pale eyes blink incessantly and he grins about him slyly with
a greedy malice.*]

ABBIE [*suddenly turning to a young girl on her right*]: Whar's
Eben?

YOUNG GIRL [*eyeing her scornfully*]: I dunno, Mrs Cabot. I
hain't seen Eben in ages. [*Meaningly*] Seems like he's spent
most o' his time t' hum since yew come.

ABBIE [*vaguely*]: I tuk his Maw's place.

YOUNG GIRL: Ay-eh. So I've heerd.

[*She turns away to retail this bit of gossip to her mother sitting
next to her.* ABBIE *turns to her left to a big stoutish middle-
aged man whose flushed face and starting eyes show the amount
of 'likker' he has consumed.*]

ABBIE: Ye hain't seen Eben, hev ye?

MAN: No, I hain't. [*Then he adds with a wink*] If yew hain't,
who would?

ABBIE: He's the best dancer in the county. He'd ought t' come
an' dance.

MAN [*with a wink*]: Mebbe he's doin' the dutiful an' walkin'
the kid t' sleep. It's a boy, hain't it?

ABBIE [*nodding vaguely*]: Ay-eh – born two weeks back –
purty's a picter –

MAN: They all is – t' their Maws. [*Then in a whisper with a
nudge and a leer*] Listen, Abbie – if ye ever git tired o' Eben,
remember me! Don't fergit now! [*He looks at her uncomprehending face for a second – then grunts disgustedly.*] Waal –
guess I'll likker agin. [*He goes over and joins* CABOT, *who
is arguing noisily with an old farmer over cows. They all
drink.*]

ABBIE [*this time appealing to nobody in particular*]: Wonder what
Eben's a-doin'? [*Her remark is repeated down the line with many
a guffaw and titter until it reaches the fiddler. He fastens his
blinking eyes on* ABBIE.]

FIDDLER [*raising his voice*]: Bet I kin tell ye, Abbie, what

Eben's doin'! He's down t' the church offerin' up prayers o' thanksgivin'. [*They all titter expectantly.*]

A MAN: What fur? [*Another titter*]

FIDDLER: 'Cause unto him a – [*he hesitates just long enough*] – brother is born!

[*A roar of laughter. They all look from* ABBIE *to* CABOT. *She is oblivious, staring at the door.* CABOT, *although he hasn't heard the words, is irritated by the laughter, and steps forward, glaring about him. There is an immediate silence.*]

CABOT: What're ye all bleatin' about – like a flock o' goats? Why don't ye dance, damn ye? I axed ye here t' dance – t' eat, drink an' be merry – an' thar ye set cacklin' like a lot o' wet hens with the pip! Ye've swilled my likker an' guzzled my vittles like hogs, hain't ye? Then dance fur me, can't ye? That's fa'r an' squar', hain't it? [*A grumble of resentment goes around, but they are all evidently in too much awe of him to express it openly.*]

FIDDLER [*slyly*]: We're waitin' fur Eben. [*A suppressed laugh*]

CABOT [*with a fierce exultation*]: T' hell with Eben! Eben's done fur now! I got a new son! [*His mood switching with drunken suddenness*] But ye needn't t' laugh at Eben, none o' ye! He's my blood, if he be a dumb fool. He's better nor any o' yew! He kin do a day's work a'most up t' what I kin – an' that'd put any o' yew pore critters t' shame!

FIDDLER: An' he kin do a good night's work, too! [*A roar of laughter*]

CABOT: Laugh, ye damn fools! Ye're right just the same, Fiddler. He kin work day an' night, too, like I kin, if need be!

OLD FARMER [*from behind the keg where he is weaving drunkenly back and forth – with great simplicity*]: They hain't many t' touch ye, Ephraim – a son at seventy-six. That's a hard man fur ye! I be on'y sixty-eight an' I couldn't do it. [*A roar of laughter, in which* CABOT *joins uproariously.*]

CABOT [*slapping him on the back*]: I'm sorry fur ye, Hi. I'd never suspicion sech weakness from a boy like yew!

OLD FARMER: An' I never reckoned yew had it in ye nuther, Ephraim. [*Another laugh*]

CABOT [*suddenly grim*]: I got a lot in me – a hell of a lot – folks don't know on. [*Turning to the* FIDDLER] Fiddle 'er up, durn ye! Give 'em somethin' t' dance t'! What air ye, an ornament? Hain't this a celebration? Then grease yer elbow an' go it!

FIDDLER [*seizes a drink which the* OLD FARMER *holds out to him and downs it*]: Here goes!

[*He starts to fiddle 'Lady of the Lake'. Four young fellows and four girls form in two lines and dance a square dance. The* FIDDLER *shouts directions for the different movements, keeping his words in the rhythm of the music and interspersing them with jocular personal remarks to the dancers themselves. The people seated along the walls stamp their feet and clap their hands in unison.* CABOT *is especially active in this respect. Only* ABBIE *remains apathetic, staring at the door as if she were alone in a silent room.*]

FIDDLER: Swing your partner t' the right! That's it, Jim! Give her a b'ar hug! Her Maw hain't lookin'. [*Laughter*] Change partners! That suits ye, don't it, Essie, now ye got Reub afore ye? Look at her redden up, will ye? Waal, life is short an' so's love, as the feller says. [*Laughter*]

CABOT [*excitedly, stamping his foot*]: Go it, boys! Go it, gals!

FIDDLER [*with a wink at the others*]: Ye're the spryest seventy-six ever I sees, Ephraim! Now, if ye'd on'y good eyesight . . .! [*Suppressed laughter. He gives* CABOT *no chance to retort, but roars*] Promenade! Ye're walkin' like a bride down the aisle, Sarah! Waal, while they's life they's allus hope, I've heerd tell. Swing your partner to the left! Gosh A'mighty, look at Johnny Cook high-steppin'! They hain't goin' t' be much strength left fur howin' in the corn lot t'morrow. [*Laughter*]

CABOT: Go it! Go it! [*Then suddenly, unable to restrain himself any longer, he prances into the midst of the dancers, scattering*

them, waving his arms about wildly.] Ye're all hoofs! Git out o'
my road! Give me room! I'll show ye dancin'. Ye're all too
soft! [*He pushes them roughly away. They crowd back toward
the walls, muttering, looking at him resentfully.*]

FIDDLER [*jeeringly*]: Go it, Ephraim! Go it! [*He starts 'Pop
Goes the Weasel', increasing the tempo with every verse until
at the end he is fiddling crazily as fast as he can go.*]

CABOT [*starts to dance, which he does very well and with tremendous
vigour. Then he begins to improvise, cuts incredibly grotesque
capers, leaping up and cracking his heels together, prancing around
in a circle with body bent in an Indian war dance, then suddenly
straightening up and kicking as high as he can with both legs. He
is like a monkey on a string. And all the while he intersperses his
antics with shouts and derisive comments*]: Whoop! Here's
dancin' fur ye! Whoop! See that! Seventy-six, if I'm a day!
Hard as iron yet! Beatin' the young 'uns like I allus done!
Look at me! I'd invite ye t' dance on my hundredth birth-
day on'y ye'll all be dead by then. Ye're a sickly generation!
Yer hearts air pink, not red. Yer veins is full o' mud an'
water! I be the on'y man in the county! Whoop! See that!
I'm a Injun! I've killed Injuns in the West afore ye was born
– an' skulped 'em, too! They's a arrer wound on my back-
side I c'd show ye! The hull tribe chased me. I outrun
'em all – with the arrer stuck in me! An' I tuk vengeance
on 'em. Ten eyes fur an eye, that was my motter!
Whoop! Look at me! I kin kick the ceilin' off the room!
Whoop!

FIDDLER [*stops playing – exhaustedly*]: God A'mighty, I got
enuf. Ye got the devil's strength in ye.

CABOT [*delightedly*]: Did I beat yew, too? Waal, ye played
smart. Hev a swig.
  [*He pours whisky for himself and* FIDDLER. *They drink. The
  others watch* CABOT *silently with cold, hostile eyes. There is
  a dead pause. The* FIDDLER *rests.* CABOT *leans against the
  keg, panting, glaring around him confusedly. In the room above,*

EBEN *get to his feet and tiptoes out the door in rear, appearing a moment later in the other bedroom. He moves silently, even frightenedly, toward the cradle and stands there looking down at the baby. His face is as vague as his reactions are confused, but there is a trace of tenderness, of interested discovery. At the same moment that he reaches the cradle,* ABBIE *seems to sense something. She gets up weakly and goes to* CABOT.]

ABBIE: I'm goin' up t' the baby.

CABOT [*with real solicitation*]: Air ye able fur the stairs? D'ye want me t' help ye, Abbie?

ABBIE: No. I'm able. I'll be down agin soon.

CABOT: Don't ye git wore out! He needs ye, remember – our son does! [*He grins affectionately, patting her on the back. She shrinks from his touch.*]

ABBIE [*dully*]: Don't – tech me. I'm goin' – up. [*She goes.* CABOT *looks after her. A whisper goes around the room.* CABOT *turns. It ceases. He wipes his forehead streaming with sweat. He is breathing pantingly.*]

CABOT: I'm a-goin' out t' git fresh air. I'm feelin' a mite dizzy. Fiddle up thar! Dance, all o' ye! Here's likker fur them as wants it. Enjoy yerselves. I'll be back. [*He goes, closing the door behind him.*]

FIDDLER [*sarcastically*]: Don't hurry none on our account! [*A suppressed laugh. He imitates* ABBIE.] Whar's Eben? [*More laughter*]

A WOMAN [*loudly*]: What's happened in this house is plain as the nose on yer face! [ABBIE *appears in the doorway upstairs and stands looking in surprise and adoration at* EBEN, *who does not see her.*]

A MAN: Ssshh! He's li'ble t' be listenin' at the door. That'd be like him.

[*Their voices die to an intensive whispering. Their faces are concentrated on this gossip. A noise as of dead leaves in the wind comes from the room.* CABOT *has come out from the porch and stands by the gate, leaning on it, staring at the sky*] *blinkingly.* ABBIE *comes across the room silently.* EBEN *does not notice her until quite near.*]

EBEN [*starting*]: Abbie!

ABBIE: Ssshh! [*She throws her arms around him. They kiss – then bend over the cradle together.*] Ain't he purty? – dead spit 'n' image o' yew!

EBEN [*pleased*]: Air he? I can't tell none.

ABBIE: E-zactly like!

EBEN [*frowningly*]: I don't like this. I don't like lettin' on what's mine's his'n. I been doin' that all my life. I'm gittin' t' the end o' b'arin' it!

ABBIE [*putting her finger on his lips*]: We're doin' the best we kin. We got t' wait. Somethin's bound t' happen. [*She puts her arms around him.*] I got t' go back.

EBEN: I'm goin' out. I can't b'ar it with the fiddle playin' an' the laughin'.

ABBIE: Don't git feelin' low. I love ye, Eben. Kiss me. [*He kisses her. They remain in each other's arms.*]

CABOT [*at the gate, confusedly*]: Even the music can't drive it out – somethin' – ye kin feel it droppin' off the elums, climbin' up the roof, sneakin' down the chimney, pokin' in the corners. . . . They's no peace in houses, they's no rest livin' with folks. Somethin's always livin' with ye. [*With a deep sigh*] I'll go t' the barn an' rest a spell. [*He goes wearily toward the barn.*]

FIDDLER [*tuning up*]: Let's celebrate the old skunk gittin' fooled! We kin have some fun now he's went. [*He starts to fiddle 'Turkey in the Straw'. There is real merriment now. The young folks get up to dance.*]

SCENE 2

[*A half-hour later – exterior –* EBEN *is standing by the gate looking up at the sky, an expression of dumb pain bewildered by itself on his face.* CABOT *appears, returning from the barn, walking wearily, his eyes on the ground. He sees* EBEN *and his whole mood immediately changes. He becomes excited, a cruel, triumphant grin comes to his lips, he strides up and slaps* EBEN *on the back. From within come the whining of the fiddle and the noise of stamping feet and laughing voices.*]

CABOT: So har ye be!

EBEN [*startled, stares at him with hatred for a moment – then dully*]: Ay-eh.

CABOT [*surveying him jeeringly*]: Why hain't ye been in t' dance? They was all axin' fur ye.

EBEN: Let 'em ax!

CABOT: They's a hull passel o' purty gals –

EBEN: T' hell with 'em!

CABOT: Ye'd ought t' be marryin' one o' 'em soon.

EBEN: I hain't marryin' no one.

CABOT: Ye might 'arn a share o' a farm that way.

EBEN [*with a sneer*]: Like yew did, ye mean? I hain't that kind.

CABOT [*stung*]: Ye lie! 'Twas yer Maw's folks aimed t' steal my farm from me.

EBEN: Other folks don't say so. [*After a pause – defiantly*] An' I got a farm, anyways!

CABOT [*derisively*]: Whar?

EBEN [*stamps a foot on the ground*]: Har.

CABOT [*throws his head back and laughs coarsely*]: Ho-ho! Ye hev, hev ye? Waal, that's a good 'un!

EBEN [*controlling himself – grimly*]: Ye'll see.

CABOT [*stares at him suspiciously, trying to make him out – a*

pause – then with scornful confidence]: Ay-eh. I'll see. So'll ye.
It's ye what's blind – blind as a mole underground. [EBEN
suddenly laughs, one short sardonic bark: 'Ha.' *A pause.* CABOT
peers at him with renewed suspicion.] What air ye hawin'
'bout? [EBEN *turns away without answering.* CABOT *grows
angry.*] God A'mighty, yew air a dumb dunce! They's
nothin' in that thick skull o' your'n but noise – like a empty
keg it be! [EBEN *doesn't seem to hear.* CABOT'S *rage grows.*]
Yewr farm! God A'mighty! If ye wa'n't a born donkey
ye'd know ye'll never own stick nor stone on it, specially
now arter him bein' born. It's his'n, I tell ye – his'n arter I
die – but I'll live a hundred jest t' fool ye all – an' he'll be
growed then – yewr age a'most! [EBEN *laughs again his
sardonic* 'Ha'. *This drives* CABOT *into a fury.*] Ha? Ye think ye
kin git 'round that someways, do ye? Waal, it'll be her'n,
too – Abbie's – ye won't git 'round her – she knows yer
tricks – she'll be too much fur ye – she wants the farm her'n
– she was afeerd o' ye – she told me ye was sneakin' 'round
tryin' t' make love t' her t' git her on yer side ... ye ... ye
mad fool, ye! [*He raises his clenched fists threateningly.*]

EBEN [*is confronting him, choking with rage*]: Ye lie, ye old
shunk! Abbie never said no sech thing!

CABOT [*suddenly triumphant when he sees how shaken* EBEN *is*]:
She did. An' I says, I'll blow his brains t' the top o' them
elums – an' she says no, that hain't sense, who'll ye git t'
help ye on the farm in his place – an' then she says yew'n me
ought t' have a son – I know we kin, she says – an' I says, if
we do, ye kin have anythin' I've got ye've a mind t'. An'
she says, I wants Eben cut off so's this farm'll be mine when
ye die! [*With terrible gloating*] An' that's what's happened,
hain't it? An' the farm's her'n! An' the dust o' the road –
that's your'n! Ha! Now who's hawin'?

EBEN [*has been listening, petrified with grief and rage – suddenly
laughs wildly and brokenly*]: Ha-ha-ha! So that's her sneakin'
game – all along! – like I suspicioned at fust – t' swaller it all

– an' me, too . . .! [*Madly*] I'll murder her! [*He springs toward the porch, but* CABOT *is quicker and gets in between.*]

CABOT: No, ye don't!

EBEN: Git out o' my road!

[*He tries to throw* CABOT *aside. They grapple in what becomes immediately a murderous struggle. The old man's concentrated strength is too much for* EBEN. CABOT *gets one hand on his throat and presses him back across the stone wall. At the same moment,* ABBIE *comes out on the porch. With a stifled cry she runs toward them.*]

ABBIE: Eben! Ephraim! [*She tugs at the hand on* EBEN'S *throat.*] Let go, Ephraim! Ye're chokin' him!

CABOT [*removes his hand and flings* EBEN *sideways full length on the grass, gasping and choking. With a cry,* ABBIE *kneels beside him, trying to take his head on her lap, but he pushes her away.* CABOT *stands looking down with fierce triumph*]: Ye needn't t've fret, Abbie, I wa'n't aimin' t' kill him. He hain't wuth hangin' fur – not by a hell of a sight! [*More and more triumphantly*] Seventy-six an' him not thirty yit – an' look whar he be fur thinkin' his Paw was easy! No, by God, I hain't easy! An' him upstairs, I'll raise him t' be like me! [*He turns to leave them.*] I'm goin' in an' dance! – sing an' celebrate! [*He walks to the porch – then turns with a great grin.*] I don't calc'late it's left in him, but if he gits pesky, Abbie, ye jest sing out. I'll come a-runnin' an', by the Eternal, I'll put him across my knee an' birch him! Ha-ha-ha! [*He goes into the house laughing. A moment later his loud 'Whoop' is heard.*]

ABBIE [*tenderly*]: Eben! Air ye hurt? [*She tries to kiss him, but he pushes her violently away and struggles to a sitting position.*]

EBEN [*gaspingly*]: T' hell – with ye!

ABBIE [*not believing her ears*]: It's me, Eben – Abbie – don't ye know me?

EBEN [*glowering at her with hatred*]: Ay-eh – I know ye – now! [*He suddenly breaks down, sobbing weakly.*]

ABBIE [*fearfully*]: Eben – what's happened t' ye – why did ye look at me 's if ye hated me?

EBEN [*violently, between sobs and gasps*]: I do hate ye! Ye're a whore – a damn trickin' whore!

ABBIE [*shrinking back horrified*]: Eben! Ye don't know what ye're sayin'!

EBEN [*scrambling to his feet and following her – accusingly*]: Ye're nothin' but a stinkin' passel o' lies. Ye've been lyin' t' me every word ye spoke, day an' night, since we fust – done it. Ye've kept sayin' ye loved me. . . .

ABBIE [*frantically*]: I do love ye! [*She takes his hand, but he flings hers away.*]

EBEN [*unheeding*]: Ye've made a fool o' me – a sick, dumb fool – a-purpose! Ye've been on'y playin' yer sneakin', stealin' game all along – gittin' me t' lie with ye so's ye'd hev a son he'd think was his'n, an' makin' him promise he'd give ye the farm and let me eat dust, if ye did git him a son! [*Staring at her with anguished, bewildered eyes*] They must be a devil livin' in ye! 'Tain't human t' be as bad as that be!

ABBIE [*stunned – dully*]: He told yew . . .?

EBEN: Hain't it true? It hain't no good in yew lyin'. . . .

ABBIE [*pleadingly*]: Eben, listen – ye must listen – it was long ago – afore we done nothin' – yew was scornin' me – goin' t' see Min – when I was lovin' ye – an' I said it t' him t' git vengeance on ye!

EBEN [*unheedingly. With tortured passion*]: I wish ye was dead! I wish I was dead along with ye afore this come! [*Ragingly*] But I'll git my vengeance, too! I'll pray Maw t' come back t' help me – t' put her cuss on yew an' him!

ABBIE [*brokenly*]: Don't ye, Eben! Don't ye! [*She throws herself on her knees before him, weeping.*] I didn't mean t' do bad t' ye! Fergive me, won't ye?

EBEN [*not seeming to hear her – fiercely*]: I'll git squar' with the old skunk – an' yew! I'll tell him the truth 'bout the son he's so proud o'! Then I'll leave ye here t' pizen each other –

with Maw comin' out o' her grave at nights – an' I'll go t'
the gold-fields o' Californi-a whar Sim an' Peter be. . . .

ABBIE [*terrified*]: Ye won't – leave me? Ye can't!

EBEN [*with fierce determination*]: I'm a-goin', I tell ye! I'll get
rich thar an' come back an' fight him fur the farm he stole –
an' I'll kick ye both out in the road – t' beg an' sleep in the
woods – an' yer son along with ye – t' starve an' die! [*He is
hysterical at the end.*]

ABBIE [*with a shudder – humbly*]: He's yewr son, too, Eben.

EBEN [*torturedly*]: I wish he never was born! I wish he'd die
this minit! I wish I'd never sot eyes on him! It's him – yew
havin' him – a-purpose t' steal – that's changed everythin'!

ABBIE [*gently*]: Did ye believe I loved ye – afore he come?

EBEN: Ay-eh – like a dumb ox!

ABBIE: An' ye don't believe no more?

EBEN: B'lieve a lyin' thief! Ha!

ABBIE [*shudders – then humbly*]: An' did ye really love me afore?

EBEN [*brokenly*]: Ay-eh – an' ye was trickin' me!

ABBIE: An' ye don't love me no more!

EBEN [*violently*]: I hate ye, I tell ye!

ABBIE: An' ye're truly goin' West – goin' t' leave me – all on
account o' him bein' born?

EBEN: I'm a-goin' in the mornin' – or may God strike me t'
hell!

ABBIE [*after a pause – with a dreadful cold intensity – slowly*]: If
that's what his comin's done t' me – killin' yewr love – takin'
ye away – my on'y joy – the on'y joy I ever knowed –
like heaven t' me – purtier'n heaven – then I hate him, too,
even if I be his Maw!

EBEN [*bitterly*]: Lies! Ye love him! He'll steal the farm fur ye!
[*Brokenly*] But 'tain't the farm so much – not no more – it's
yew foolin' me – gittin' me t' love ye – lyin' yew loved me
– jest t' steal . . .!

ABBIE [*distractedly*]: He won't steal! I'd kill him fust! I do love
ye! I'll prove t' ye –

EBEN [*harshly*]: 'Tain't no use lyin' no more. I'm deaf t' ye!
[*He turns away.*] I hain't seein' ye agen. Good-bye!

ABBIE [*pale with anguish*]: Hain't ye even goin' t' kiss me – not
once – arter all we loved – ?

EBEN [*in a hard voice*]: I hain't wantin' t' kiss ye never again!
I'm wantin' t' forgit I ever sot eyes on ye!

ABBIE: Eben! – ye mustn't – wait a spell – I want t' tell ye . . .

EBEN: I'm a-goin' in t' git drunk. I'm a-goin' t' dance.

ABBIE [*clinging to his arm – with passionate earnestness*]: If I
could make it – 's if he'd never come up between us – if I
could prove t' ye I wa'n't schemin' t' steal from ye – so's
everythin' could be jest the same with us, lovin' each other
jest the same, kissin' an' happy the same's we've been happy
all along – if I could do it – ye'd love me agen, wouldn't ye?
Ye'd kiss me agen? Ye wouldn't never leave me, would ye?

EBEN [*moved*]: I calc'late not. [*Then shaking her hand off his
arm – with a bitter smile*] But ye hain't God, be ye?

ABBIE [*exultantly*]: Remember ye've promised! [*Then with
strange intensity*] Mebbe I kin do one thin' God does!

EBEN [*peering at her*]: Ye're gittin' cracked, hain't ye? [*Then
going toward door*] I'm a-goin' t' dance.

ABBIE [*calls after him intensely*]: I'll prove t' ye! I'll prove I
love ye better'n . . . [*He goes in the door, not seeming to hear. She
remains standing where she is, looking after him – then she finishes
desperately.*] Better'n everythin' else put t'gether!

SCENE 3

Just before dawn in the morning – shows the kitchen and CABOT'S *bedroom.*

[*In the kitchen, by the light of a tallow candle on the table,* EBEN *is sitting, his chin propped on his hands, his drawn face blank and expressionless. His carpet bag is on the floor beside him. In the bedroom, dimly lighted by a small whale-oil lamp,* CABOT *lies asleep.* ABBIE *is bending over the cradle, listening, her face full of terror, yet with an undercurrent of desperate triumph. Suddenly, she breaks down and sobs, appears about to throw herself on her knees beside the cradle, but the old man turns restlessly, groaning in his sleep, and she controls herself, and, shrinking away from the cradle with a gesture of horror, backs swiftly toward the door in rear and goes out. A moment later she comes into the kitchen and, running to* EBEN, *flings her arms about his neck and kisses him wildly. He hardens himself, he remains unmoved and cold, he keeps his eyes straight ahead.*]

ABBIE [*hysterically*]: I done it, Eben! I told ye I'd do it! I've proved I love ye – better'n everythin' – so's ye can't never doubt me no more!

EBEN [*dully*]: Whatever ye done, it hain't no good now.

ABBIE [*wildly*]: Don't ye say that! Kiss me, Eben, won't ye? I need ye t' kiss me arter what I done! I need ye t' say ye love me!

EBEN [*kisses her without emotion – dully*]: That's fur good-bye. I'm a-goin' soon.

ABBIE: No! No! Ye won't go – not now!

EBEN [*going on with his own thoughts*]: I been a-thinkin' – an' I hain't goin' t' tell Paw nothin'. I'll leave Maw t' take vengeance on ye. If I told him, the old skunk'd jest be stinkin' mean enuf to take it out on that baby. [*His voice showing emotion in spite of him*] An' I don't want nothin' bad t' happen t' him. He hain't t' blame fur yew. [*He adds with a certain queer pride.*] An' he looks like me! An', by God, he's mine! An' some day I'll be a-comin' back an' –

ABBIE [*too absorbed in her own thoughts to listen to him – pleadingly*]: They's no cause fur ye t' go now – they's no sense – it's all the same's it was – they's nothin' come b'tween us now – arter what I done!

EBEN [*something in her voice arouses him. He stares at her a bit frightenedly*]: Ye look mad, Abbie. What did ye do?

ABBIE: I – I killed him, Eben.

EBEN [*amazed*]: Ye killed him?

ABBIE [*dully*]: Ay-eh.

EBEN [*recovering from his astonishment – savagely*]: An' serves him right! But we got t' do somethin' quick t' make it look 's if the old skunk'd killed himself when he was drunk. We kin prove by 'em all how drunk he got.

ABBIE [*wildly*]: No! No! Not him! [*Laughing distractedly*] But that's what I ought t' done, hain't it? I oughter killed him instead! Why didn't ye tell me?

EBEN [*appalled*]: Instead? What d'ye mean?

ABBIE: Not him.

EBEN [*his face grown ghastly*]: Not – not that baby!

ABBIE [*dully*]: Ay-eh!

EBEN [*falls to his knees as if he'd been struck – his voice trembling with horror*]: Oh, God A'mighty! A'mighty God! Maw, whar was ye, why didn't ye stop her?

ABBIE [*simply*]: She went back t' her grave that night we fust done it, remember! I hain't felt her about since. [*A pause. EBEN hides his head in his hands, trembling all over as if he had the ague. She goes on dully.*] I left the piller over his little face. Then he killed himself. He stopped breathin'. [*She begins to weep softly.*]

EBEN [*rage beginning to mingle with grief*]: He looked like me. He was mine, damn ye!

ABBIE [*slowly and brokenly*]: I didn't want t' do it. I hated myself fur doin' it. I loved him. He was so purty – dead spit 'n' image o' yew. But I loved yew more – an' yew was goin' away – far off whar I'd never see ye agen, never kiss ye, never feel ye pressed agin me agen – an' ye said ye hated me fur havin' him – ye said ye hated him an' wished he was dead – ye said if it hadn't been fur him comin' it'd be the same's afore between us.

EBEN [*unable to endure this, springs to his feet in a fury, threatening her, his twitching fingers seeming to reach out for her throat*]: Ye lie! I never said – I never dreamed ye'd – I'd cut off my head afore I'd hurt his finger!

ABBIE [*piteously, sinking on her knees*]: Eben, don't ye look at me like that – hatin' me – not after what I done fur ye – fur us – so's we could be happy agen –

EBEN [*furiously now*]: Shut up, or I'll kill ye! I see yer game now – the same old sneakin' trick – ye're aimin' t' blame me fur the murder ye done!

ABBIE [*moaning – putting her hands over her ears*]: Don't ye, Eben! Don't ye! [*She grasps his legs.*]

EBEN [*his mood suddenly changing to horror, shrinks away from her*]: Don't ye tech me! Ye're pizen! How could ye – t' murder a pore little critter – Ye must've swapped yer soul t' hell! [*Suddenly raging*] Ha! I kin see why ye done it! Not the lies ye jest told – but 'cause ye wanted t' steal agen – steal the last thin' ye'd left me – my part o' him – no, the hull o' him – ye saw he looked like me – ye knowed he was all mine – an' ye couldn't b'ar it – I know ye! Ye killed him fur bein' mine! [*All this has driven him almost insane. He makes a rush past her for the door – then turns –shaking both fists at her, violently.*] But I'll take vengeance now! I'll git the Sheriff! I'll tell him everythin'! Then I'll sing, 'I'm off to Californi-a!' an' go – gold – Golden Gate – gold sun – fields o' gold in the West! [*This last he half-shouts, half-croons incoherently, suddenly breaking off passionately.*] I'm a-goin' fur the Sheriff t' come an' git ye! I want ye tuk away, locked up from me! I can't stand t' luk at ye! Murderer an' thief 'r not, ye still tempt me! I'll give ye up t' the Sheriff!

[*He turns and runs out, around the corner of house, panting and sobbing, and breaks into a swerving sprint down the road.*]

ABBIE [*struggling to her feet, runs to the door, calling after him*]: I love ye, Eben! I love ye! [*She stops at the door weakly, swaying, about to fall.*] I don't care what ye do – if ye'll on'y love me agen! [*She falls limply to the floor in a faint.*]

SCENE 4

About an hour later. Same as Scene 3. Shows the kitchen and CABOT'S *bedroom. It is after dawn. The sky is brilliant with the sunrise.*

[*In the kitchen,* ABBIE *sits at the table, her body limp and exhausted, her head bowed down over her arms, her face hidden. Upstairs,* CABOT *is still asleep, but awakens with a start. He looks toward the window and gives a snort of surprise and irritation – throws back the covers and begins hurriedly pulling on his clothes. Without looking behind him, he begins talking to* ABBIE, *whom he supposes beside him.*]

CABOT: Thunder 'n' lightnin', Abbie! I hain't slept this late in fifty year! Looks 's if the sun was full riz a'most. Must've been the dancin' an' likker. Must be gittin' old. I hope Eben's t' wuk. Ye might've tuk the trouble t' rouse me, Abbie. [*He turns – sees no one there – surprised.*] Waal – whar air she? Gittin' vittles, I calc'late. [*He tiptoes to the cradle and peers down – proudly.*] Mornin', sonny. Purty's a picter! Sleepin' sound. He don't beller all night like most on 'em. [*He goes quietly out the door in rear – a few moments later enters kitchen – sees* ABBIE – *with satisfaction.*] So thar ye be. Ye got any vittles cooked?

ABBIE [*without moving*]: No.

CABOT [*coming to her, almost sympathetically*]: Ye feelin' sick?

ABBIE: No.

CABOT [*pats her on shoulder. She shudders*]: Ye'd best lie down a spell. [*Half-jocularly*] Yer son'll be needin' ye soon. He'd ought t' wake up with a gnashin' appetite, the sound way he's sleepin'.

ABBIE [*shudders – then in a dead voice*]: He hain't never goin' t' wake up.

CABOT [*jokingly*]: Takes after me this mornin'. I hain't slept so late in –

ABBIE: He's dead.

CABOT [*stares at her – bewilderedly*]: What –?

ABBIE: I killed him.

CABOT [*stepping back from her – aghast*]: Air ye drunk – 'r crazy – 'r – ?

ABBIE [*suddenly lifts her head and turns on him – wildly*]: I killed him, I tell ye! I smothered him. Go up an' see if you don't b'lieve me!

[CABOT *stares at her a second, then bolts out the rear door, can be heard bounding up the stairs, and rushes into the bedroom and over to the cradle.* ABBIE *has sunk back lifelessly into her former position.* CABOT *puts his hand down on the body in the crib. An expression of fear and horror comes over his face.*]

CABOT [*shrinking away – trembling*]: God A'mighty! God A'mighty. [*He stumbles out the door – in a short while returns to the kitchen – comes to* ABBIE, *the stunned expression still on his face – hoarsely.*] Why did ye do it? Why? [*As she doesn't*

answer, he grabs her violently by the shoulder and shakes her.]
I ax ye why ye done it! Ye'd better tell me 'r –

ABBIE [*gives him a furious push which sends him staggering back and springs to her feet – with wild rage and hatred*]: Don't ye dare tech me! What right hev ye t' question me 'bout him? He wa'n't yewr son! Think I'd have a son by yew? I'd die fust! I hate the sight o' ye an' allus did! It's yew I should've murdered, if I'd had good sense! I hate ye! I love Eben. I did from the fust. An' he was Eben's son – mine an' Eben's – not your'n!

CABOT [*stands looking at her dazedly – a pause – finding his words with an effort – dully*]: That was it – what I felt – pokin' round the corners – while ye lied – holdin' yerself from me – sayin' ye'd a'ready conceived. . . . [*He lapses into crushed silence – then with a strange emotion.*] He's dead, sart'n. I felt his heart. Pore little critter! [*He blinks back one tear, wiping his sleeve across his nose.*]

ABBIE [*hysterically*]: Don't ye! Don't ye! [*She sobs unrestrainedly.*]

CABOT [*with a concentrated effort that stiffens his body into a rigid line and hardens his face into a stony mask – through his teeth to himself*]: I got t' be – like a stone – a rock o' jedgement! [*A pause. He gets complete control over himself – harshly.*] If he was Eben's, I be glad he air gone! An' mebbe I suspicioned it all along. I felt they was somethin' onnateral – somewhars – the house got so lonesome – an' cold – drivin' me down t' the barn – t' the beasts o' the field. . . . Ay-eh. I must've suspicioned – somethin'. Ye didn't fool me – not altogether, leastways – I'm too old a bird – growin' ripe on the bough. . . . [*He becomes aware he is wandering, straightens again, looks at* ABBIE *with a cruel grin.*] So ye'd liked t' hev murdered me 'stead 'o him, would ye? Waal, I'll live to a hundred! I'll live t' see ye hung! I'll deliver ye up t' the jedgement o' God an' the law! I'll git the Sheriff now. [*Starts for the door.*]

ABBIE [*dully*]: Ye needn't. Eben's gone fur him.

CABOT [*amazed*]: Eben – gone fur the Sheriff?

ABBIE: Ay-eh.

CABOT: T' inform agen ye?

ABBIE: Ay-eh.

CABOT [*considers this – a pause – then in a hard voice*]: Waal, I'm thankful fur him savin' me the trouble. I'll git t' wuk. [*He goes to the door – then turns – in a voice full of strange emotion.*] He'd ought t' been my son, Abbie. Ye'd ought t' love me. I'm a man. If ye'd loved me, I'd never told no Sherid on ye, no matter what ye did, if they was t' brile me alive!

ABBIE [*defensively*]: They's more to it nor yew know, makes him tell.

CABOT [*dryly*]: Fur yewr sake, I hope they be. [*He goes out – comes around to the gate – stares up at the sky. His control relaxes. For a moment he is old and weary. He murmurs despairingly.*] God A'mighty, I be lonesomer'n ever! [*He hears running footsteps from the left, immediately is himself again.* EBEN *runs in, panting exhaustedly, wild-eyed and mad-looking. He lurches through the gate.* CABOT *grabs him by the shoulder.* EBEN *stares at him dumbly.*] Did ye tell the Sheriff?

EBEN [*nodding stupidly*]: Ay-eh.

CABOT [*gives him a push away that sends him sprawling – laughing with withering contempt*]: Good fur ye! A prime chip o' yer Maw ye be! [*He goes toward the barn, laughing harshly.* EBEN *scrambles to his feet. Suddenly* CABOT *turns – grimly threatening.*] Git off this farm when the Sheriff takes her – or, by God, he'll have t' come back an' git me fur murder, too!

[*He stalks off.* EBEN *does not appear to have heard him. He runs to the door and comes into the kitchen.* ABBIE *looks up with a cry of anguished joy.* EBEN *stumbles over and throws himself on his knees beside her – sobbing brokenly.*]

EBEN: Fergive me!

ABBIE [*happily*]: Eben! [*She kisses him and pulls his head over against her breast.*]

EBEN: I love ye! Fergive me!

ABBIE [*ecstatically*]: I'd fergive ye all the sins in hell fur sayin' that! [*She kisses his head, pressing it to her with a fierce passion of possession.*]

EBEN [*brokenly*]: But I told the Sheriff. He's comin' fur ye!

ABBIE: I kin b'ar what happens t' me – now!

EBEN: I woke him up. I told him. He says, 'Wait 'til I git dressed.' I was waiting. I got to thinkin' o' yew. I got to thinkin' how I'd loved ye. It hurt like somethin' was bustin' in my chest an' head. I got t' cryin'. I knowed sudden I loved ye yet, an' allus would love ye!

ABBIE [*caressing his hair – tenderly*]: My boy, hain't ye?

EBEN: I begun t' run back. I cut across the fields an' through the woods. I thought ye might have time t' run away – with me – an' –

ABBIE [*shaking her head*]: I got t' take my punishment – t' pay fur my sin.

EBEN: Then I want t' share it with ye.

ABBIE: Ye didn't do nothin'.

EBEN: I put it in yer head. I wisht he was dead! I as much as urged ye t' do it!

ABBIE: No. It was me alone!

EBEN: I'm as guilty as yew be! He was the child o' our sin.

ABBIE [*lifting her head as if defying God*]: I don't repent that sin! I hain't askin' even God t' fergive that!

EBEN: Nor me – but it led up t' the other – an' the murder ye did, ye did 'count o' me – an' it's my murder, too, I'll tell the Sheriff – an' if ye deny it, I'll say we planned it t'gether – an' they'll all b'lieve me, fur they suspicion everythin' we've done, an' it'll seem likely an' true to 'em. An' it is true – way down – I did help ye – somehow.

ABBIE [*laying her head on his – sobbing*]: No! I don't want yew t' suffer!

EBEN: I got t' pay fur my part o' the sin! An' I'd suffer wuss leavin' ye, goin' West, thinkin' o' ye day an' night, bein' out when yew was in . . . [*Lowering his voice*] 'R bein' alive when yew was dead. [*A pause*] I want t' share with ye, Abbie – prison 'r death 'r hell 'r anythin'! [*He looks into her eyes and forces a trembling smile.*] If I'm sharin' with ye, I won't feel lonesome, leastways.

ABBIE [*weakly*]: Eben! I won't let ye! I can't let ye!

EBEN [*kissing her – tenderly*]: Ye can't he'p yerself. I got ye beat fur once!

ABBIE [*forcing a smile – adoringly*]: I hain't beat – s'long's I got ye!

EBEN [*hears the sound of feet outside*]: Ssshh! Listen! They've come t' take us!

ABBIE: No, it's him. Don't give him no chance to fight ye, Eben. Don't say nothin' – no matter what he says. An' I won't, neither. [*It is* CABOT. *He comes up from the barn in a great state of excitement and strides into the house and then into the kitchen.* EBEN *is kneeling beside* ABBIE, *his arm around her, hers around him. They stare straight ahead.*]

CABOT [*stares at them, his face hard. A long pause – vindictively*] Ye make a slick pair o' murderin' turtle-doves! Ye'd ough t' be both hung on the same limb an' left thar t' swing in the breeze an' rot – a warnin' t' old fools like me t' b'are their lonesomeness alone – an' fur young fools like ye t' hobble their lust. [*A pause. The excitement returns to his face, his eyes snap, he looks a bit crazy.*] I couldn't work today. I couldn't take no interest. T' hell with the farm! I'm leavin' it! I've turned the cows an' other stock loose! I've druv 'em into the woods whar they kin be free! By freein' 'em, I'm freein' myself! I'm quittin' here today! I'll set fire t' house an' barn an' watch 'em burn, an' I'll leave yer Maw t' haunt the ashes, an' I'll will the fields back t' God, so that nothin' human kin never touch 'em! I'll be a-goin' to Californi-a t' jine Simeon an' Peter – true sons o' mine if they be dumb

204

fools – an' the Cabots 'll find Solomon's Mines t'gether! [*He suddenly cuts a mad caper.*] Whoop! What was the song they sung? 'Oh, Californi-a! That's the land fur me.' [*He sings this – then gets on his knees by the floor-board under which the money was hid.*] An' I'll sail thar on one o' the finest clippers I kin find! I've got the money! Pity ye didn't know whar this was hidden so's ye could steal . . . [*He has pulled up the board. He stares – feels – stares again. A pause of dead silence. He slowly turns, slumping into a sitting position on the floor, his eyes like those of a dead fish, his face the sickly green of an attack of nausea. He swallows painfully several times – forces a weak smile at last.*] So – ye did steal it!

EBEN [*emotionlessly*]: I swapped it t' Sim an' Peter fur their share o' the farm – t' pay their passage t' Californi-a.

CABOT [*with one sardonic laugh*]: Ha! [*He begins to recover. Gets slowly to his feet – strangely.*] I calc'late God give it to 'em – not yew! God's hard, not easy! Mebbe they's easy gold in the West, but it hain't God's gold. It hain't fur me. I kin hear His voice warnin' me agen t' be hard an' stay on my farm. I kin see His hand usin' Eben t' steal t' keep me from weakness. I kin feel I be in the palm o' His hand, His fingers guidin' me. [*A pause – then he mutters sadly.*] It's a-goin' t' be lonesomer now than ever it war afore – an' I'm gittin' old, Lord – ripe on the bough. . . . [*Then stiffening*] Waal – what d'ye want? God's lonesome, hain't He? God's hard an' lonesome! [*A pause. The* SHERIFF *with two men comes up the road from the left. They move cautiously to the door. The* SHERIFF *knocks on it with the butt of his pistol.*]

SHERIFF: Open in the name o' the law! [*They start.*]

CABOT: They've come fur ye. [*He goes to the rear door.*] Come in, Jim! [*The three men enter.* CABOT *meets them in doorway.*] Jest a minit, Jim. I got 'em safe here. [*The* SHERIFF *nods. He and his companions remain in the doorway.*]

EBEN [*suddenly calls*]: I lied this mornin', Jim. I helped her do it. Ye kin take me, too.

ABBIE [*brokenly*]: No!

CABOT: Take 'em both. [*He comes forward – stares at* EBEN *with a trace of grudging admiration.*] Purty good – fur yew! Waal, I got t' round up the stock. Good-bye.

EBEN: Good-bye.

ABBIE: Good-bye.

[CABOT *turns and strides past the men – comes out and around the corner of the house, his shoulders squared, his face stony, and stalks grimly toward the barn. In the meantime the* SHERIFF *and men have come into the room.*]

SHERIFF [*embarrassed*]: Waal – we'd best start.

ABBIE: Wait. [*Turns to* EBEN.] I love ye, Eben.

EBEN: I love ye, Abbie. [*They kiss. The three men grin and shuffle embarrassedly.*]

EBEN [*to the* SHERIFF]: Now. [*He takes* ABBIE'S *hand.*] Come. [*They go out the door in rear, the men following, and come from the house, walking hand-in-hand to the gate.* EBEN *stops there and points to the sunrise sky.*] Sun's a-risin'. Purty, hain't it?

ABBIE: Ay-eh. [*They both stand for a moment looking up raptly in attitudes strangely aloof and devout.*]

SHERIFF [*looking around at the farm enviously – to his companions*]: It's a jim-dandy farm, no denyin'. Wish I owned it!

CURTAIN